# Study skills for
## *foundation degrees*

WITHDRAWN

# Study skills for
# *foundation degrees*

**Dorothy Bedford and Elizabeth Wilson**

 **David Fulton** Publishers

David Fulton Publishers Ltd
The Chiswick Centre, 414 Chiswick High Road, London W4 5TF

www.fultonpublishers.co.uk

www.onestopeducation.com

First published in Great Britain in 2006 by David Fulton Publishers

10  9  8  7  6  5  4  3  2  1

David Fulton Publishers is a division of Granada Learning Limited.

*British Library Cataloguing in Publication Data*
A catalogue record for this book is available from the British Library.

ISBN-10: 1 84312 464 5
ISBN-13: 978 1 84312 464 1

Typeset by FiSH Books, Enfield, Middx.
Printed and bound in Great Britain

# Contents

# Acknowledgements

Grateful acknowledgement is made to the following sources for permission to reproduce material:

Southern England Consortium for Credit Accumulation and Transfer (SEEC) for permission to reproduce the credit level descriptors for HE1, HE2 and HE3 from *Credit Level Descriptors for Further and Higher Education* (January 2003), in Appendix I.

CIPD Enterprises Ltd (www.cipd.co.uk) for permission to reproduce the Sample Personal Development Plan (Figure 9.2).

BBC (www.bbc.co.uk/webwise) for permission to reproduce the 'How to unravel a URL' (Table 3.1).

Franklin Covey Co. for permission to reproduce the Time Management Matrix (Figure 8.1).

QCA for permission to reproduce the National Qualifications Framework Table 1.1).

Thanks also go to Charles Bedford, Peter Davies and Tracey Riseborough for their help and encouragement.

We should also like to thank all the foundation degree staff and students who contributed enthusiastically to this project. Particular thanks go to Hilary Budd, Marilyn Dooley-Gailis, Colette Harvey, Jake Hodges, Jane Hudson, Sandra Kendall, Maria Panayi, Angela Scollan, Julie Scott-Browne, Jon Swinfield, Glynis Thomson, Melissa Unguneanu and Christina Whittingham.

# 1 So you want to study for a foundation degree? Useful preparation prior to starting your course

## ▓ What is a foundation degree?

Foundation degrees have only been around since 2001, so you may not know much about them. This section aims to expand your knowledge. Foundation degrees are unique in that they integrate academic and work-based learning to provide an employment-related higher education (HE) qualification. They are validated by universities to ensure that they meet high academic standards but are designed and delivered in partnership with employers, to equip people with the relevant knowledge and skills for work.

## Which subjects are offered?

Foundation degrees cover a broad range of vocational areas that aim to equip you with the knowledge, skills and understanding relevant to your current or future work. They are designed in partnership with employers and the range of subject areas is growing all the time. Subjects include agriculture, art and design, business, computing, education, engineering, health and care, hospitality and tourism, media, music, performing arts and sport. Many other areas are covered, as you will find out by completing the task below.

### ACTIVITY

Log on to the Foundation Degree Forward website (www.fdf.ac.uk). If you don't have access to a computer at home or at work, or are not confident in using the internet, ask for help from your local library. Look at the range of foundation degree programmes available in the vocational areas that interest you and make a list of those offered that are close to where you currently live or work. You can cross-check this information against the UCAS (University Central Admissions Service) website (www.ucas.ac.uk).

## Where can I study for a foundation degree?

Foundation degrees are usually delivered by colleges and universities and sometimes by large employers. The list you will have drawn up above will have given you an idea of those courses being offered near to where you work or live. You may also want to look at full-time courses offered away from home if you are thinking of starting a new career. All universities and colleges have their own websites where you can access information about the courses and ask for a prospectus and course information sheets.

**ACTIVITY**

Look again at the list you made of the courses that interest you. Find out the websites and addresses where the courses are offered and send off for their details. Universities and colleges often have a number of different physical locations; you will need to find out where these courses are actually delivered. If the course offers an open day or a chance to meet the tutors informally, put the date in your diary and go along.

## How long will it take me?

This depends on the mode of study you choose. A full-time course will usually take two years to complete; part-time courses will take longer, but they offer the opportunity to continue working while you study. Many courses have flexible teaching arrangements involving part-time or evening attendance at college, distance learning or learning via the internet. The next section (p.3) will help you to decide which course is the right one for you at this time.

## Which qualifications do I need to start a foundation degree?

You don't necessarily need traditional academic qualifications to gain entry to a course. You can get onto a foundation degree using your work experience and any academic or vocational qualifications you have, like A levels, BTEC Nationals, NVQs and Apprenticeships. It's worth remembering that any commercial and industrial experience you have could be as important as educational qualifications. The institution delivering the foundation degree will decide if you're eligible, and they'll decide using a system called APEL (Accreditation of Prior Experiential Learning), which uses your work experience to judge your ability. You will be able to find out more about APEL in 'Making an application' below.

**ACTIVITY**

Look again at the courses you have selected. What do they state are the entry requirements? Do you meet these? If not, you will need to consider making an application through APEL.

## So is a foundation degree a 'proper' degree?

Foundation degrees are valuable qualifications in their own right. Successful students will have the right to use the letters 'FdA', for arts-based subjects, or 'FdSc', for science-based subjects, after their name. A foundation degree allows you to demonstrate that you are disciplined in your approach to work and can think independently; and employers will know that you are not only academically and theoretically qualified, but that you've got the useful practical experience they need. A foundation degree is a qualification at the intermediate level in the Framework for Higher Education Qualifications and is worth 240 credit points, 120 at HE level 1 and a further 120 at HE level 2. The qualification frameworks are complicated, but the table overleaf should give you an indication of where foundation degrees fit in to both the Framework for Higher Education Qualifications, and the revised National Qualifications Framework.

## What progression opportunities exist after I have achieved a foundation degree?

The last chapter of this book covers your options in some detail, including progressing to other professional qualifications and to more senior posts at work. However, in academic terms you can progress to an honours degree through further study. This will require you to study for an additional 120 credit points at HE level 3. This will usually take around a year if you study full-time and more if you study on a part-time basis, depending on the programme. All foundation degrees are required to have a designated honours degree to which you can progress; this is known as 'articulation', but you can take your 240 credit points to any university or higher education institution.

## Is this the right course for me at this stage?

### What are your main reasons for wanting to study?

Awareness of your motivation and your personal goals can make a real difference in helping you to complete the degree programme. Most students have difficulties with some aspects of the course. Looking back at your initial motivation can help you overcome any problems you may be faced with. As an adult you are studying in addition to many other commitments. It can be difficult to keep going, especially if you are studying part-time over a number of years, and it's not realistic to expect the rest of your life to be put on hold.

**TABLE 1.1** Qualification frameworks showing foundation degrees (Source: QCA revised National Qualifications Framework 2004)

| National Qualifications Framework | | Framework for Higher Education Qualification levels (FHEQ) |
|---|---|---|
| Original levels (with examples of qualifications you may have) | Revised levels | |
| 5<br>Level 5 NVQ | 8<br>Specialist awards | D (doctoral)<br>doctorates |
| 5<br>Level 5 NVQ | 7<br>Level 7 Diploma | M (masters)<br>masters degrees, postgraduate certificates and diplomas |
| 4<br>Level 4 NVQ<br>BTEC Higher National Diploma/Certificate | 6<br>Level 6 Diploma | H (HE3) (honours)<br>bachelors degrees, graduate certificates and diplomas |
| 4<br>Level 4 NVQ<br>BTEC Higher National Diploma/Certificate | 5<br>Level 5 BTEC Higher National Diploma | I (HE2) (intermediate)<br>diplomas of higher education and further education, foundation degrees, higher national diplomas |
| 4<br>Level 4 NVQ<br>BTEC Higher National Diploma/Certificate | 4<br>Level 4 Certificate | C (HE1) (certificate)<br>certificates of higher education |
| 3<br>BTEC National Diploma/Certificate<br>Level 3 NVQ/GNVQ<br>A levels<br>Modern Apprenticeships | | |
| 2<br>BTEC First Diploma/Certificate<br>Level 2 NVQ/GNVQ<br>O level/GCSEs grades A*–C | | |
| 1<br>Level 1 Certificate<br>Level 1 NVQ<br>O level/GCSEs grades D–G | | |
| Entry<br>Entry-level Certificate in Adult Literacy | | |

**ACTIVITY**

What are your own main reasons for wanting to study for a foundation degree? Make a list in your notebook and keep it to remind you of your initial motivation. You might want to add to your list when you look at the comments by successful foundation degree students below. Save this list; we'll be using it again in Chapter 2.

Peter, a student on a foundation degree in Information Technology, summarises what he has gained from his foundation degree:

'The benefits, professionally, of being able to say that I have a degree are immeasurable. The more I learn, the more self-assured I become. The programme has raised my confidence. I have found my voice and can now speak out.'

'I have new credibility at work, with my input being an intrinsic element of IT decision-making and strategic planning. For example, I am invited to give my input at senior management meetings and my view is seen as an expert opinion rather than "what Peter thinks". I am looking forward to more doors opening and making further progress in my career.'

The *Foundation Degree Task Force Report to Ministers* (DfES 2004) identifies a number of reasons why students may wish to study for a foundation degree:

● flexible delivery;
● a second chance for mature students;
● to get a specific job;
● career enhancement;
● access to higher education;
● employer recognition;
● the fact that it is shorter and cheaper than an honours degree.

The same report suggests that the demand for foundation degrees comes mainly from:

- people in work or their employers seeking to develop and upgrade work-force skills;
- people in work or their employers seeking vocationally oriented progression routes from work-based level 3 programmes;
- people with non-traditional entry qualifications seeking a route to a higher education qualification;
- people wanting a change of occupation;
- employers seeking to fill skill gaps, develop new job roles or meet regulatory requirements. (p.11)

That's the theory; the question you need to ask yourself is: Am I sufficiently interested in the subject and motivated to attend college regularly and participate actively in my own learning? If so, read on.

## Can I afford it?

To answer this question you first need to know how much the course is going to cost you. From September 2006, universities and colleges will be able to charge up to £3,000 a year for their courses. Fees are decided by each of the institutions, so you'll need to check costs with them. If you are going to do your foundation degree while you work, some of the costs may be covered by your employer. As a foundation degree student, you may find that your costs are lower than those for honours degree students, and you will complete your learning sooner, but you will be entitled to the same financial help. For instance, there is currently a loan available to eligible students to cover tuition fees, or you could be eligible for a non-repayable grant or bursary. You can get helpful information on fees and funding from the student services department of the academic institution or from www.direct.gov.uk/studentfinance and www.aimhigher.ac.uk

Remember, the cost of your degree will be more than just the fees; you need to take into account the extra travel, recommended books (although you may be able to share books with other students, there will still be some you need to buy), stationery and even extras like tea and coffee in the refectory. Some courses also require that you pay towards material costs or purchase a kit of equipment, so check carefully all the costs involved. Don't forget any indirect costs such as extra childcare and the loss of any salary or overtime payments.

Now you need to think about how you are going fund your study. If you are employed, will your employer pay a proportion or all of your tuition, and other, costs? It is important to find out whether they will support you financially before enrolling on your course. If your employer has a staff development budget consider when it is best to ask for funding – at the beginning of a financial year, or at the end, when there might be some money left over? Do your homework, and remember to put the business case for your degree in terms of any project work that will relate directly to your current job. You may be asked to repay part of the costs if you leave during, or shortly after, your foundation degree – but that is a decision you may need to take if you get offered a better job.

**ACTIVITY**

If you are employed and want to take a foundation degree to enhance your career, make a list of all the costs involved over the length of the degree. Find out who you need to ask for support – is it your line manager, training and development officer or the managing director – and the procedure involved. Now write down your personal objectives and how the course will directly benefit the organisation. Don't skimp on this last point. Finally, either fill in the staff development request form or write to the appropriate person making a specific request for funding. Good luck.

## Can I commit the time to study?

The final section of this chapter will look at planning the year ahead; and there is a whole chapter on time management techniques later in the book. However, in our experience, being able to keep up with the workload – particularly if you are working full-time as some foundation degree students do – is what concerns students most. You need to ask yourself if your current situation is flexible enough to take on this major commitment, as you need to commit not only to class time but also to study time and to do assignments. Remember, everybody works at a different pace.

Jon, a student on the foundation degree in Teaching and Learning, admits that:

'The most difficult thing is motivating
myself to study away from the classroom and finding a quiet
personal space to get my head down and learn. My tutors have
been brilliant helping me out with this, sharing study skills and
techniques and helping me to devise a study programme. I have
discovered that the best time to study is early in the
morning before the kids get up!'

> 'When people ask me how I manage to fit everything in,
> working as a teaching assistant, studying and bringing up my
> family, I have to be honest and say that it can be very challenging.
> However, I am determined to become a teacher and this is
> what I have to do to achieve that.'

## Different modes of study

To a large extent, the delivery method depends on the course you choose and the academic institution behind it. Many full-time and part-time courses now also offer opportunities for distance and on-line learning. This increases your flexibility, which is especially useful if you don't live or work near the university or college.

### Part-time study

Part-time study has a major advantage in that it can be fitted in around your work schedule and other commitments. If you continue working you can apply what you learn in your workplace, so both you and your employer benefit. You can also continue to earn, as Kate, an art and design student explains:

> 'I couldn't afford to give up work to study full-time,
> so this foundation degree gives me the opportunity to work and
> learn at the same time for a qualification that is absolutely
> relevant to my job.'

### Full-time study

A considerable number of foundation degree students choose to study full-time, either going on to university or college after studying for a level 3 qualification, such as A levels or a National Diploma. A full-time foundation degree usually takes two years to complete. If you study full-time you will be required to have a work placement as part of your course. In that way, when you graduate you can go into work fully prepared for the industry, with relevant, valuable skills and knowledge. The balance of the work-based and academic study depends on the course you choose and the academic institution that is running it.

## Do I have the academic skills needed to be successful?

That question is what this book is all about. However, the foundation degree students we teach identify a lack of confidence in being able to reach the academic level required. The good news is that many colleges and universities have excellent support services to help you develop your academic skills – after all, it is in their interests for you to be successful. Have a look at the website and the prospectus of any institutions you are interested in; you will probably see a range of services from additional learning support (ALS) for students with learning difficulties such as dyslexia and dyscalculia, as well as screening to identify if additional support is needed for English, numeracy and IT. Support for students can be offered on a one-to-one and small-group basis. Many colleges and universities also offer seminars on study skills, which could be worth attending in addition to working through this book.

## ◾ Making an application

Once you have decided what you want to study, you need to apply for a place.

### Applying for a full-time foundation degree

If you intend to study full-time, you will apply through UCAS, the Universities and Colleges Admissions Service. This means filling out a standard form and writing a personal statement. UCAS provides plenty of advice on how to fill in the application form, including a list of dos and don'ts. You can apply on paper, or on-line at the UCAS website (www.ucas.ac.uk). You can apply for up to six courses, or just one if you are sure of the institution at which you want to study.

Normally, applications need to be sent to UCAS between 1 September of the year before you want to start your course and 15 January of the year in which you intend to start, so if you want to study full-time then you need to think ahead.

### Applying for a part-time foundation degree

If you want to study part-time, or on a flexible learning course, you will need to make a direct application to the appropriate academic institution. They will use a form very like the UCAS form, but the deadlines will probably be far more flexible, so check with each institution. Some further education colleges offering higher education courses also recruit directly.

---

**ACTIVITY**

By now you should have all the application forms. Make a photocopy of each form and practise filling it in. It is really helpful to show this copy to someone whom you trust and listen to their feedback. When you've made any amendments on the draft, complete the original form, take a photocopy of it and put it in the post.

### The APEL process

As you know, there are no set entry requirements for a foundation degree as the academic institution offering the course will decide if you are qualified. However, if you do not have a level 3 qualification – A levels, NVQ 3 or equivalent – then it is likely that you will have to demonstrate that you are able to benefit from studying at this level through the process known as APEL. This recognises the skills and experience you already possess. All colleges and universities vary in their procedures for APEL, but they usually involve putting together a portfolio of evidence, an interview and a review of your past experience. You should contact the admissions tutor for more information and guidance.

We have been talking about APEL to gain access to a foundation degree; however, you can also ask for prior experience or certificated learning to give exemptions for particular modules. For example, if you are working as a teaching assistant and have a specialist teaching assistant course certificate in supporting literacy, then it may be possible to ask for exemptions from a module on literacy strategy. In this case your tutor would probably look at what you have learned on your specialist teaching assistant course and the level it covered. This is clearly different from using APEL to join a course if you don't have 'traditional' level 3 qualifications, but it is certainly worth considering.

## ▤ Creating a support network of family, friends and colleagues

### Support from family and friends

You will have to sit down and discuss your decision with your family and friends. These people will form part of your informal support team. The more they understand what you are undertaking, the more they will be supportive when the going gets tough. You should not underestimate the impact that your goal will have on those around you. For example, try not to lose contact with your friends. It's hard enough to stay connected to people given our already busy lives, so make the time to speak with them. A number of our students have said that by studying they have acted as a role model for their children.

Maybe others you live with could, for example, do more of the chores, especially during term time. By agreeing some ground rules at the beginning of your course you should be able to share out some of your current responsibilities. Sometimes, spending more money will save you time, like ordering food on-line and arranging for it to be delivered, or employing someone to help in the house or garden. Consider any options that will make your life easier; but, of course, you need to make sure you can afford it.

### Finding a workplace mentor

As you will now be aware, a key characteristic of foundation degrees is the integration of academic studies and work-based learning. In many cases your foundation degree programme will require you to have the support of a workplace mentor. Even if this is not required by your course you should consider approaching a member of staff at your workplace whom you respect, and ask if they would be able to mentor you through your foundation degree. The ideal mentor is usually a more experienced colleague who already holds a qualification at a similar, or more advanced, level and who has practical experience of the job. This may be your line manager, but not necessarily. You need to find a person whom you can be open and honest with about any difficulties you may be having with the course.

Mentors have a key role in facilitating work-based learning; they help you to make the link between the theoretical knowledge you acquire from academic study and your professional practice. Regular meetings with your mentor can focus on making these links and encourage you to reflect on your personal and professional development. Mentors may also carry out observations of you at work and provide feedback on your performance.

In addition to helping you relate academic learning and theoretical knowledge to your job, the right mentor can:

- use their knowledge of the workplace to help you access information that can assist in the completion of your assignments and projects;
- put you in touch with individuals with 'expert' knowledge of the organisation;
- support you by helping to resolve problems and provide encouragement and advice.

Although this is a time-consuming process for both you and your mentor, many students report how useful the relationship has been to both parties. Jane, a student on the Childcare and Early Years degree states that:

'There are a number of factors that have contributed to me successfully embarking on the second year of the programme: I have been fortunate to have an excellent mentor at my school, and the continuing support of my family, workplace and the college. I definitely feel more valued at work, particularly by my head teacher, who is also my workplace mentor. My self-confidence has grown due to my increased knowledge.'

**ACTIVITY**

If you are employed, identify a colleague you think would make a good mentor. Check whether your course offers any guidance for mentors – many universities and colleges offer an induction handbook and even a mentoring qualification. Arrange a meeting to see your potential mentor and ask if they are prepared to become involved in your learning.

## Preparing a space to study

Now your application is in, you will need to make the most of your valuable study time, so finding a place that is conducive to study is important. The ideal solution is a quiet room where you can shut the door and not be disturbed. However, not everyone is this fortunate. If you are able to have a designated area at home, consider how your circumstances match up against the following checklist:

- A desk or table, large enough to spread out your books and files and to accommodate a laptop or PC if necessary.
- A comfortable chair, which supports your back and is designed for use with a computer, if appropriate.
- Adequate heating and ventilation – you don't want to be so warm that you doze off or so cold that you can't concentrate.
- Appropriate lighting, preferably natural light, and a reading lamp you can turn on at night.
- Storage space – a bookcase or cupboard where you can easily put your work away – and don't forget a waste paper basket.
- Access to a computer; this is ideal, but you may be able to use a computer at your workplace or college. If you need to share a home computer with others then access times need to be negotiated.
- A good supply of stationery items such as coloured pens, pencils, highlighter pens, ruler, calculator, post-it notes, stapler, hole punch, files, dividers and paper.

Although you may have negotiated with members of your family to have uninterrupted study time, you may need to hang a 'Do not disturb' sign on the door or take the phone off the hook. Research shows that most students study best in a quiet environment. If you find that the radio or TV improves your concentration, keep the volume low. With experience you will be able to decide where and how you study best.

## ■ Some top tips for success

Julie has a list of advice for potential students:

> 'I would suggest you get the full support of
> your employer; you need to have a suitable mentor who has
> the time to help you with your assignments. You will also need a
> very supportive and understanding family, a computer and lots of
> spare time. The only thing I would have done differently would be to
> get it in writing that my employer was going to support me
> financially throughout the two years.'

Jane suggests: 'I would advise a student to familiarise themselves with using their computer, particularly if they are a parent,' while Marcus advises: 'You should be aware of how much time will be needed to devote to study beyond college attendance.'

### Creating a study schedule

Find out about the proposed study workload for students, term dates and (when you start) deadlines. This information should all be part of your induction to the course.

### ACTIVITY

Buy a diary or year planner, or learn to use the calendar function on your computer, such as Microsoft Outlook. Academic year diaries are usually on sale in the summer. Get all deadlines into your diary and begin to consider how these fit in with your work and other responsibilities. It is also a good idea to pencil in birthdays, holidays, work deadlines and other academic and family commitments.

### Start to think about your time management

We have written a whole chapter on this, but you can make a start now. While many people do the bulk of their studying during the weekends, you should still try to do some of your coursework during the week, so that you don't feel too overwhelmed. Maybe you can do some reading during your commute to work or lunch break. Getting a degree demands a lot of effort and time, but when you graduate we are sure you will agree that it was worth it. Some ideas we've been given by students include those listed below:

- Stop checking your home and work e-mail so often. Pick times at which you will check your e-mail, possibly three times – morning, afternoon and the evening.
- Instead of driving to work, consider taking the train, tube or bus. This may take a little longer but you can use that time to study or to relax.
- Always carry with you some work that can be fitted in to unexpected free time, perhaps a photocopy of some recommended reading or the latest assignment question.
- Decide on what will be your regular study times. It's easy to delay starting if study is to be fitted in anytime. You will need to think about when you are at your best; are you a lark or an owl?

## And finally...

Once you have your place, you may well be wondering if you made the right decision. We address the issues adults have returning to learn in the next chapter – thoughts like: 'Am I doing the right thing?' 'Will this really get me somewhere in my career?' and 'Will I be any good at it?' are natural. This is a big step in your life, but we are sure you will find that everyone in your study group will feel anxious, especially in the first couple of weeks. Our advice is not to over-think your decision; just do what you can to prepare in advance, then take each day at a time.

The last words in this chapter should go to Jon:

> 'I am so glad that I made this step; it is one of the biggest steps of my life. I was very fearful of study and not being able to cope with the course, but with the support of my family, classmates and excellent tutors I have now completed my first year. I am further up the career ladder in my new job, but most importantly I am following my vocational calling and I am on my way to becoming a teacher.'

> 'If you are thinking about embarking on a foundation degree my advice would be to go for it, at least give it a try, it won't be as daunting as you think and the rewards can be fantastic.'

## ■ Websites to visit for more information

www.aimhigher.ac.uk – this is a comprehensive site covering a wide range of issues for potential higher education students, including careers guidance; universities and colleges; applying for courses; student finance; and student life.

www.dfes.gov.uk/studentsupport – for useful information on available student support packages.

www.direct.gov.uk/studentfinance – for useful information on funding and fees.

www.fdf.ac.uk – this is the website of Foundation Degree Forward and lists foundation degrees by subject areas, courses and institutions.

www.foundationdegree.org.uk – a useful source of further information about foundation degrees.

www.hotcourses.co.uk – this site lists subject areas, courses and institutions and is worth checking to cross-reference.

www.ucas.ac.uk – this site contains essential information on applying for full-time foundation degree courses and lists of foundation degrees.

## ■ References

DfES (2004) *Foundation Degree Task Force Report to Ministers.* Nottingham: Department for Education and Skills.

# 2 Learning as an adult

In the last chapter you examined what motivated you to consider committing yourself to a foundation degree. You thought about all the necessary steps you needed to confirm it was the right decision and to get accepted onto a course. This is often the place where students begin to experience doubts about the new career path they have chosen. Whether you are experiencing doubt or not, this is the point in your decision-making where it makes a lot of sense to look backwards as well as forwards. This chapter will introduce you to some theory and techniques. These will help you look critically at how you got to where you are now; your previous experiences of learning, including your time at school. This should help you to get to where you want to be. The intention is that you will look at this chapter periodically as there is a lot to take in.

In the past, education was, in the main, associated with what was learned at school. Few adults expected to continue learning after they had left school. However, in the last few years there have been considerable changes of thought. Now most adults recognise the claim that learning is key to achieving our full potential. In fact, the Campaign for Learning (www.campaign-for-learning.org.uk) considers that, 'human beings are uniquely adapted to learn and we have the ability to do so throughout our lives'.

## How do we learn?

### Thinking about adult learning

An important part of preparing for any kind of study is to identify how you learned what you already know. In that way you can build on success. You are always learning, not only at school; just think how much you learned before you started school. The following section should help you to understand more about yourself. Additionally, it will provide you with some useful information to help you to complete any personal development modules of your foundation degree. You will find out more about this in Chapter 9.

For at least the last century, researchers, psychologists and teachers have proposed theories of learning and suggested teaching styles to assist learning.

More recently there has been a specific interest in adult learning. But, in spite of the vast number of books, journal articles and research papers devoted to the subject, we are still a long way from understanding the key differences in learning as a child and learning as an adult. Indeed, Stephen Brookfield (1995) identified a number of assumptions that we hold about adult learning. You may agree with some of them; others you may take issue with.

- It is part of adult behaviour to be self-directed.
- Adults explain what their educational needs are to their tutor.
- Adult learners work well on their own.
- Adult learners need to know why they are learning something and will decide if it is relevant to them.
- Adult learners are practical problem-solvers.
- Adult learners have accumulated life experiences.
- The adult learning process and practice are unique.

However, we have to be careful not to assume that theories about adult learning apply equally to everyone. According to Brookfield (1995) we should not treat all adult learners as being the same simply because they are not in school; we have to remember that the differences of class, culture, ethnicity, personality, cognitive style (knowing and understanding), learning patterns, life experiences and gender among adults are more significant than the fact that they are not children or adolescents. We have tried to bear this in mind while we have been writing this book. There will be times when you disagree with something that we have suggested. We see this as a positive step; it shows that you are developing as a critical reader.

## Levels of learning

Research suggests that there are three levels of learning;

- cognition: knowing and understanding – for example, you watched the demonstration and now know how to create tables in the spreadsheet package Excel;
- conception: deep understanding that can be recalled – for example, three weeks, or even years later, you can still create tables and could do it again unaided;
- application: understanding and use of the knowledge – for example, not only have you learned but you have also added to that knowledge and are able to explain it to someone else.

Ideally, we are always working towards the application level.

## Gaining knowledge

We also need to think about the ways in which we gain knowledge. We have a tendency to assume that all learning is conscious and the result of applying ourselves in school or college. But what about learning to ride a bicycle, for instance? Much of that was quite unconscious; maybe we watched someone carefully. That type of learning is referred to as tacit. Procedural knowledge is what we gain from doing something repeatedly. Explicit knowledge is what you learn in your lectures or by reading a book. You can see that to be successful you need to be learning in all three ways.

Peter Honey and Alan Mumford (1992) suggested that people vary in their preferred learning styles. They identified four types of learner.

- Activists, who involve themselves fully in the new experience and prefer fieldwork, observations and practical 'hands-on' activities.
- Reflectors, who stand back to ponder experiences and observe from different perspectives, and prefer brainstorming, journal keeping and recording logs.
- Theorists, who adapt and integrate observations into complex but logically sound theories, and prefer lectures, research papers, books and written examples.
- Pragmatists, who like to try out new ideas, theories and techniques to see if they work in practice, and prefer simulations, case studies and homework.

Anna advises that you 'identify your learning style. It will inform the way you learn and how you can improve weaker areas.'

## Different forms of intelligence

To help you understand yourself even better, you might also like to consider Howard Gardner's theory of multiple intelligences. What he claimed, in 1983, was that intelligence is not only about being academically clever, that is, good at mathematics, reading and writing, but also about using life experiences.

To support his argument he used examples of other sorts of knowledge that people acquire, sometimes to an exceptional standard, without necessarily having any academic learning at all. One example was that of the Puluwat navigators of the Caroline Islands in the South Seas, who successfully navigate their way safely through thousands of islands with no written text. First they have to be able to remember exactly where certain stars rise and set. They use this knowledge combined with other factors such as where the sun is, what the waves feel like as they go over them, if they change course, how strong the wind is and the weather conditions. They also use skills in steering and sailing and an ability to estimate the depth of the water without a measure.

Another example Gardner gave was of a small child, not yet able to read, who could recite the entire Koran by heart. On the basis of his discoveries he proposed that there is a range of different intelligences. In his original theory there were seven, the last one in this list (see Activity box below) is a recent addition and it is likely more will be added as his evidence accumulates.

Each of these intelligences can be linked to preferences in the way you process and use information.

---

**ACTIVITY**

Consider the extent to which you can demonstrate the following intelligences and think of some examples. You will probably find you fit into more than one category.

- Linguistic/verbal: the ability to use language in written and oral forms.
- Logical/mathematical: the ability to reason logically and manipulate numbers.
- Visual/spatial: the ability to recognise and produce visual images.
- Kinaesthetic: the ability to co-ordinate the body and to use it to express and achieve goals.
- Musical: the ability to recognise and produce music.
- Naturalist: the ability to recognise and interact with the natural world.
- Interpersonal: the ability to understand the motives, emotional states and intentions of others.
- Intrapersonal: the ability to understand one's own motives, characteristics, strengths and weaknesses.

---

## Types of learning

Considerable research has been carried out, notably by Jarvis (1992), into adult learners' recollections of the way they learn. His research suggests that the way you confront a learning experience determines what you learn. He found that there are three states:

### Non-learning

- making the same mistakes even when they are pointed out;
- thinking that you already know what is being taught;
- thinking it is not worth paying attention;
- rejecting what you have been taught.

### Non-reflective learning

- changing learning behaviour and gaining new skills without really understanding what you have done and why.

*Reflective learning*

- Deep changes in understanding as a result of reflecting objectively, relating the learning to previous experience. You will find more about reflective learning in Chapter 9.

David Kolb (1984) described four phases in what he called a 'learning cycle'. His ideas have probably had more influence on how people think about learning than any others. He visualised these phases as stages that we work through:

- planning study tasks, taking account of the way you prefer to learn;
- carrying out the work;
- reflecting on the experience;
- thinking about what helped you learn and what got in the way.

## ■ Building on previous experience

As we have already mentioned, research suggests that our learning as adults is quite different from when we were children. Maybe this is a good thing, because some of you may carry quite negative memories of your early learning experiences. Janet, a foundation degree student in Travel and Tourism, confessed, 'Studying was new to me; I didn't do particularly well at school, so I have had to learn how to study'; and Roberta said, 'I wish I'd studied harder at school and not waited till now'.

---

**ACTIVITY**

Try to examine your learning experiences in full-time education using the 'fishbone' technique (Figure 2.1):

- draw a horizontal line to represent the spine of the fish;
- draw lines at right angles to the spine to represent aspects of your experiences in full-time education;
- positive experiences go above the spine, negative below;
- the longer the line you draw at right-angles the more positive or negative the experience;
- write a few words on each of the lines to identify what they represent.

---

For example, if you looked forward to seeing your friends at school that would be represented by a long line above and at right-angles to the spine. If you hated school dinners there would be a long line at right-angles below the spine. Complete the fishbone by identifying issues, subjects, ways of learning and so on. Are there more negative than positive points?

| Negative | Positive |
|---|---|
| Emotional ties | Nearer to work |
| Leaving lovely garden | Beautiful view and quiet location |
| Securing a mortgage | Excellent transport system |
| Bartering prices | Looking at other people's ideas |
| Seeing people around and hearing nothing | Choosing property to suit requirements |
| Leaving a secure environment | Nearer to friends |
| Leaving good neighbours | More cultural opportunities |
| Leaving good doctors | Excellent shopping |
| Packing | Choosing decor for new home |
| Unpacking | Good medical facilities |

**FIGURE 2.1** Positive and negative points about moving house 'fishbone' analysis

**ACTIVITY**

Look at your fishbone analysis. List all the negative points. Divide them into groups under three headings:

- issues that are no longer important; for example, you did not like the mathematics teacher;
- issues you have learned to cope with; for example, you were too shy to make many friends, but it is not important now because you have made some very good friends;
- issues that you did not deal with, but will have to if you are going to achieve your foundation degree; for instance, you hated homework.

Now let's look at the list of things you have to deal with. It is no good pretending that they will go away. They can become real barriers for you. Ask yourself:

- Why was this negative experience?
- What can I do to change it?
- When will I do this?
- Who can help me? Don't forget your family, friends and tutors; you do not have to do this alone.

**ACTIVITY**

Now return to the 'fishbone' and make a list of all the positive points that you think apply to you as a learner. These are really important for you. Now add what you see as additional positive experiences that you have gained since leaving school.

What you add here will vary according to a whole range of possible influences such as your age, gender, responsibilities, employment, cultural background, ethnicity and so on. For example, you passed your driving test, which enabled you to look further afield for employment. You did a first aid course and are now an Appointed Person at work. Don't undervalue your experience; it is all evidence of your learning and will help you to think positively about what you bring with you.

## Motivation for further study

While you are thinking about the experiences you have gained and the difference from your learning experiences at school, this is a good place to be honest with yourself about your reasons for studying again.

**ACTIVITY**

Remind yourself of the list in Chapter 1. To what extent do you think the following reasons are true or false for you?

- To make friends or maintain your friendship group.
- To meet external expectations – your employer expects you to upgrade to keep your job.
- You want to learn so that you can help others – such as gaining life-saving certification qualifications.
- You want to gain professional advancement – promotion or change of job.
- You need to be stimulated.
- You are personally interested in the area of study and want to know more.
- Personal improvement.
- A second chance to achieve what you had failed to achieve before.
- A chance to do something that you had previously not had the opportunity to do.
- The chance to complete something you had previously started.

Some of these reasons may not be sufficient to carry you through difficult times. For example, the success of the first two is dependent on other factors. Enrolling on a course to make friends might work and you might be very happy and motivated, but on the other hand you might not. Enrolling on a course because your employer expects you to may be enough to keep you interested, but you might just decide it would be better to change jobs. Enrolling because you need stimulating could be sufficient motivation for you to complete a short creative course, but will it be enough for something longer and more demanding? If you have identified a motive that might not be strong enough to see you through difficult times, look again at the list. Is there something more positive that applies?

Mary, a second-year foundation degree student, commented,

> 'After leaving school at 16 I worked in
> retail for some time. Even at a managerial level I felt
> the need to change direction. So I took a job as a library
> assistant and within a short while a position in IT became
> available. I was fortunate that my aptitude for IT was discovered
> and I was subsequently singled out for a promotion internally. I
> received some training, but it soon became apparent that
> I would benefit from a professional qualification.'

## Managing your morale

Starting a degree is nearly always exciting. Your confidence has been boosted by getting a place on the course, you have bought the books, organised your work space and things could not be better. Be prepared, however, for times when your morale is low; there is nothing more damaging to your studies. It can make you doubt yourself so much that you find you are just sitting and staring at your work. Worse still, you can't be bothered to study and you look for more pleasant things to do, or even decide not to continue your degree. Low morale is a lot more common than you might think and can be caused by a whole range of factors.

We have made a list of what we see as being the most common causes of low morale and then offer some solutions that have worked for us. You might be very fortunate and never experience the following concerns; others of you will need to dip into this part of the chapter from time to time to remind yourself how to cope with the low moments.

Causes of low morale at the beginning of your course:

- change to your routines, such as different hours, new travel arrangements to organise;
- too much information to absorb, such as new routes, new surroundings, new names and faces, texts to buy, rooms to find. Virginia tells us, 'It has felt like

a long time since my brain has had this type of workout; it's a very big shock to the system';

- cultural changes to make, such as being part of a very large organisation; forming different types of relationships with peers and tutors; new ideas.

Personal causes of low morale:

- loss of confidence in your ability to meet the standards needed to complete the degree;
- not feeling in control of your learning;
- not feeling that you are part of the academic community; you fear that your ideas, your way of speaking, your appearance and so on set you apart; you want to 'belong';
- you feel that your studies are separating you from your family and friends.

Day-to-day crises that can lower your morale:

- feeling that the work is far too difficult and you do not know where to begin;
- being unable to make any sense of a set text you have been asked to read;
- technology letting you down; your printer stops working for no apparent reason;
- a friend or family member needs you and you have work to finish for a deadline;
- a tutor, a part of a course or a set text is really boring;
- you get a poor mark for an assignment;
- you worry unnecessarily about a slightly lower grade and start to get obsessed by your marks;
- the initial excitement of starting the course is over and it is all becoming too 'samey'; this is often referred to as the 'midway blues'.

The following is a list of things that can improve your morale.

- the satisfaction of finishing a set task or a difficult text – this is particularly satisfying if you can achieve your goal ahead of the deadline;
- being proud of a result that was better than expected;
- getting your work organised and planning your time;
- doing your filing and knowing you have set up a good system;
- completing forms and dealing with administrative tasks;
- focusing on what you have achieved so far; in Hilary's words, 'It's valuable to look back on lower-level work to indicate how far you have progressed';
- learning about something that is really interesting;

- realising you know enough to express a point of view, and feeling confident enough to do so. Mukoto tells us, 'I have started to build on my past experience – and my confidence has also improved';
- learning how to express yourself in seminars;
- being brave enough to present a paper and then being praised;
- realising that there are things you can now achieve that you had only dreamed about;
- feeling that you are part of the student body; you have a good support group and have people you can talk to about your concerns;
- you know how to find information;
- discovering that most of your initial causes of low morale were common to your fellow students;
- finding there are people you can talk to about your problems, such as the student counsellor or your tutor;
- your friends and family support you and are – often secretly – proud of you.

Sometimes it is only a case of changing perspective and looking at the same thing in a different way. Think positively.

Now you are motivated, excited and enthusiastic, a word of caution: one of the key differences between you as an adult learner and you as a child – apart from the fact that school is compulsory, but *you* made this choice to study – is that although you may bring a whole range of life experience, you also have life's 'baggage'.

Modern psychology has identified that the way in which humans interact with one another will determine the success of the relationship. Eric Berne took this idea further with his theory of Transactional Analysis (Berne 1968). He claimed that verbal communication, most often face-to-face, is at the centre of human relationships. He also said, using the ideas of Sigmund Freud from the early part of the twentieth century, that each person is made up of three states: Parent, Adult and Child.

This work is important for you as you embark on learning as an adult. This is because there is a tendency for all students, no matter how mature, to immediately assume that they should adopt a childlike or inferior attitude in their relationship to their tutors. Although this could be seen as a mark of respect, it is not helpful for either party as it can result in the student becoming dependent on the tutor.

Berne's Transactional Analysis theory can be summed up as follows below. As you read it, think carefully about your interactions with other adults. Think about ways in which you can work to make the relationship with your tutors that of two adults and not adult–child.

Berne claims that the Parent is our ingrained voice of authority; it is the conditioning, learning and attitudes we gained when we were young. This part of us was formed by external events and the influences of authority figures in our lives. We can change it but, for Berne, this is easier said than done.

The Child is formed by our internal reactions and feelings about the external events. This is the seeing, feeling, emotional body of information in us. When we are overcome with anger or despair, the Child is in control.

The Adult is our ability to think and determine actions for ourselves. For Berne this begins to form from when we are about ten months old and is the way we keep the Parent and Child under control. If we want to change anything about our Parent or Child it has to be done through the Adult.

He identified the following physical and verbal clues that we can use to detect which role or 'ego-state' we are in:

Parent:

● physical: angry or impatient body language, finger-pointing, patronising gestures;
● verbal: judgemental or critical words: 'always', 'never', 'for once and for all'.

Child:

● physical: emotional, despair, temper tantrums, rolling eyes, shrugging gestures, teasing, delight, squirming, giggling;
● verbal: baby talk, 'I'm gonna', 'I don't care', superlatives, words to impress.

Adult:

● physical: attentive, interested, straightforward, tilted head, non-threatened;
● verbal: Why? What? How? Who? Where? When? comparative expressions, reasoned statements, 'I think', 'I realise'.

When you are trying to identify an ego-state, words are only part of the story; much of the meaning is para-linguistic – the way the words are said – and in facial expressions. There are no rules as to the success of one state over another; some people get results by being dictatorial – Parent to Child – or by having temper tantrums – Child to Parent. But for a balanced approach, Adult to Adult is recommended. Transactional Analysis is, effectively, a language within a language. When you start to look to others to support you in your learning, try examining the ego-state you are displaying and whether it is the most effective mode of behaviour for you.

In this chapter you have considered how people learn, analysed the way you like to learn, looked positively at your life experiences and constructively at some of the obstacles that might get in the way of you achieving a foundation degree. You are now ready to 'go for it'. The Campaign for Learning offers some final advice:

- relax: stress reduces your ability to learn; take deep breaths and relax your shoulders before starting to learn – formally or informally;

- remember: all the good experiences that made you feel proud – the birth of a child, a sporting achievement and so on;

- replenish: a balanced diet keeps your brain in top gear; proteins and plenty of water help the memory; carbohydrates tend to make us sluggish;

- absorb: remember how you prefer to learn and be positive; we are often as successful as we expect to be. Above all, enjoy.

## Recommended reading

Gray, D., Cundell, S., Hay, D. and O'Neill, J. (2004) *Learning through the Workplace: A Guide to Work-based Learning.* London: Nelson Thornes.

Jarvis, M. (2005) *The Psychology of Effective Teaching and Learning.* London: Nelson Thornes.

## References

Berne, E. (1968) *Games People Play: The Psychology of Human Relationships.* London: Penguin.

Brookfield, S. (1995) 'Adult learning: an overview'. *International Encyclopaedia of Education.* Oxford: Pergamon Press.

Campaign for Learning (www.campaign-for-learning.org.uk).

Gardner, H. (1983) *Frames of Mind.* New York: HarperCollins.

Honey, P. and Mumford, A. (1992) *The Manual of Learning Styles.* Maidenhead: Peter Honey.

Jarvis, P. (1992) *The Paradoxes of Learning.* San Francisco, CA: Jossey-Bass.

Kolb, D. (1984) *Experiential Learning: Experience as a Source of Learning and Development.* Englewood Cliffs, NJ: Prentice-Hall.

# 3 Making good notes and reading effectively

Now that you are studying for a degree you will be expected to find out a lot of information for yourself. Looking at what your educational institution can provide to help you is a really important step. Additionally, finding, recording and retrieving the mass of information available is a fundamental part of studying for any higher-level qualification. This chapter aims to identify ways to help you do this; by looking at the sources of information you should have access to, ways of recording what you have found and offering some useful hints to make things as manageable as possible.

Textbooks, the internet, handouts, workplace policies and documents, lectures, presentations, demonstrations, observations and conversations can all be sources of useful information that you may need at a later date. Perhaps you can think of others. Some of this information will have been given to you by your tutors; the rest you will be finding out for yourself.

## The learning resources centre

Libraries are often called learning resources centres (LRC) because not only are there books, journals, newspapers and so on, but there are also computers, videos, DVDs and other helpful aids. They provide a convenient place to work with a quiet atmosphere. This will encourage you to study because all the resources you need are conveniently to hand.

There is, however, a tremendous variety in the quality and quantity of resources a university or college library provides. You may also need to check out your local public library or see if the course provider has an arrangement with a nearby university for you to use their facilities. General guides giving opening hours, procedures for borrowing and returning and other essential information should be given to you when you enrol. Check that you have them. You will usually need a membership card so also have some passport-sized photographs available if possible.

## Some useful tips for studying in your learning resources centre

- Have a goal to achieve; you may be preparing in advance for a lecture or researching for an assignment. Be clear about what you need to find out.
- Decide what you can do in the time available. You may have 30 minutes or a whole afternoon. Colette states that, 'You really need to spend time on reading and studying; maybe you can change your hours of work to make it easier to get to the LRC'.
- Do not be too ambitious; it is better to complete a task than to leave half-way through and feel frustrated.
- Try to find a workplace that suits you and is near to the resources you will need.
- Avoid sitting with friends; arrange to meet them at a particular time for a break and a chat about the work.
- Get into the habit of using your learning resources centre from the start of your course, it will pay dividends later on.

## What you can expect to find in your learning resources centre?

- books, journals and reference sources, both in print and electronic format to support your studies;
- open-access computing suites offering a range of software;
- video, multimedia, slide and audio collections;
- media services for photocopying, binding and equipment loan;
- video, and sound recording and editing facilities;
- e-mail and internet access;
- study skills guides;
- staff available to help with all of the above.

## Getting to know your learning resources centre

Before you get started take a little time to get to know the layout of your learning resources centre.

**ACTIVITY**

On your first visit, introduce yourself to the librarian. Let them know you are starting a foundation degree. You might need to explain what that entails. Find out:

- if a tour of your learning resources centre is provided;
- where the 'help-desks' are and who you can ask for help;
- how the library system works; is it computerised or do they still have a card index system? How does one access the library catalogue (OPAC, Online Public Access Catalogue);
- what specialist resources exist for your studies, such as videos, DVDs and slides;
- where the reference section is for specialist journals, encyclopaedias, dictionaries, directories, government reports etc.;
- if you get software or media support, and where;
- from the information desk if you can check books out at a self-issue terminal.
- Do not be too proud to ask for help, especially if the system is unfamiliar. You can waste a lot of time and get very frustrated. Go with a colleague; two heads are often better than one; and make notes of the useful things you found out.

## Finding a book

Your course or module handbook will have a bibliography at the end or you may be given a reading list. This is a list of texts that the tutors who designed the course consider will help you to understand the teaching and to explore ideas in greater depth. It helps to study some of these suggestions before you start a module.

**ACTIVITY**

Select any book from your bibliography, preferably one that sounds interesting, and using the following information, see if you can find it. Make a note of the steps you took.

### How books are arranged

You could browse the shelves. Although there is a chance you might find something really useful, this can be very time-consuming. You will have noticed as you looked along the shelves that books are divided into sections and arranged in numerical order. This is called the Dewey Decimal Classification (DDC) system, the most widely used information classification system in the world.

In this system knowledge is organised into ten main divisions and these are divided into a further ten groups. For example:

300 is Social Sciences

- 310 Statistics
- 330 Economics
- 340 Law
- 380 Commerce

500 Pure Sciences

- 510 Mathematics

You should note that reference books are usually in a separate section; they can be used while you are in the library but cannot be taken away.

### Using the library catalogue or OPAC

Most libraries have OPAC (Online Public Access Catalogue) to help you find the texts you want. These can be accessed from any computer with an internet connection as well as from the learning resources centre itself, they are easy to use because they give on-screen instructions. The library catalogue is organised in three main ways, for example:

| | |
|---|---|
| Subject Index | abbeys–butterflies |
| Author Catalogue | Aaron–Armitage |
| Classified Catalogue | 001–120 |

The Subject Index tells you where to look in the library but does not list the books. The Author Catalogue lists some possible titles and tells you the book number. The Classified Catalogue tells you what the book is if you know its number.

## Using journals and newspapers

Your learning resources centre will have available past and present copies of a large number of journals and newspapers. It makes sense to check them all out at the beginning of your course. Journals usually have a summary at the beginning of each article – the abstract – telling you what it is all about. A quick look at the abstracts will tell you if the journal could be useful to you. It is not a good idea to decide on the basis of the journal titles alone; they can be very misleading.

**ACTIVITY**

Make a note of all the journals that might help in your studies.

## The internet and electronic resources

More and more students are beginning to rely on the internet for inspiration and ideas; in fact, finding relevant material on the web that you can use in your studies is very exciting.

The internet is a vast source of information connecting millions of computers around the world; computers belonging to governments, companies, universities, colleges, schools, libraries, museums, galleries, science laboratories and many others. All these computers hold information, some of which is free for you to use. Many universities and colleges have arrangements with each other to allow students the widest access to reliable information. Make sure you know which universities you can link to.

Some websites are designed specifically to help you learn new things by providing information for coursework, essays and assignments. Others help you keep up to date with new developments in your specialist subject. If you want to find out something quickly there are dictionaries, encyclopaedias and reference works to help you.

## Using the internet

Everyone thinks they know how to search the internet, so why is it sometimes so difficult for us to find the right information? It could be one of the following:

- using the wrong search tool for the job;
- not planning a good search strategy;
- not choosing the best keywords.

### Finding the right search tool

There are three main types of internet search tools available, all of which offer something slightly different from the others. You will need to understand more about these tools before you can decide which is most suitable for your purpose.

### Search engines

When you are using a search engine you are using a tool that searches millions (if not billions) of websites on every subject imaginable. They are handy if you want to find a specific piece of information. Google is one such search engine.

### Web directories

When you use a web directory you can look through (or browse) thousands of websites organised under subjects. They are useful if you want popular sites as well as serious ones. Directories are built by editors in a commercial company. Lycos is an example of a web directory.

## Subject gateways

In general, gateways are the best starting points for exploring what is available on the internet to support college work. Subject gates are trustworthy too. They are tools built by experts from universities and colleges to enable you to search thousands of websites organised under subject headings. An example of a subject gateway is the Resource Discovery Network (www.rdn.ac.uk/news/index.html).

## Planning your search strategy

When you are searching you need to break down your topic and identify your key concepts or ideas.

---

**ACTIVITY**

Make a list of the possible phrases or words you could use to find someone who sells Jaguar cars. Try to use phrases you might read on a web page.

---

Have you used terms that could be ambiguous? Are you looking for jaguar the animal or Jaguar the car? How can you use other terms to restrict your search? You might say 'Jaguar cars', 'Jaguar car dealer', or 'Jaguar car showroom', for example. If you wanted to bring up the results for a particular country, or part of one, you would also have to restrict your search. We will look at how to do this later on in the section (p.35).

## Choosing the right keywords

Imagine you want to find out about poverty in working families in south-east England after World War II. Your key concepts are 'poverty', 'working families', 'south-east' England, '1945'.

Once you have identified your concepts you need to list the key words you associate with each topic. Some may have only one, others may have a number. For example:

Poverty: low income, financial deprivation, lack of money, poor
Working families: working-class, employed
south-east England: southern counties
1945: you will have to define your limits here, otherwise you could end up looking at data about the last 60 years; perhaps you could limit the search to between 1945 and 1960.

Depending on the focus of your work there may be other keywords you might use.

*Tips for conducting searches*

- Read the directions at each site carefully; the way to make a search varies from one search engine to another.
- Check your spelling.
- Use words that are similar (synonyms) or have different spellings.
- If your strategy is still not working, try using a different phrase. Try another directory or search engine; no two search engines are the same.
- Try the option available on some search engines such as AltaVista or Google to find documents similar or related to one of your relevant hits.
- Use the Boolean operators, AND, NOT, OR. Using these will find titles that contain all the words you have typed, for example 'human AND resource AND management' will find items containing all three words. Using NOT will help to reduce hits if you have too many. For example, 'Farm NOT Machinery'. The operator OR can also widen your search, for example 'English OR British Moths'. Putting double quotes "–" at the beginning and end of a phrase limits the search, e.g. "human resource management" will only find items that contain the whole phrase.

**ACTIVITY**

Try these examples and see how many hits you get, and see how different combinations produce different results:

- graphic design
- graphic AND design
- graphic NOT design
- graphic OR design
- "graphic design"

## Judging the quality of the information

There is so much information on the internet that a lot of what is available is not relevant for you and may not be of the quality you require. Consider how the internet compares with a library. In a library, any book you find has been checked at least three times by different people: the author checks the work, then an editor double checks, then a publisher decides if it is good enough to publish, maybe a reviewer also commented on it, and lastly a librarian checked to see if it was good enough for the library. On the internet no quality checks are required. So how can you check the quality of information?

Think like a detective. Ask three questions: 'Who?', 'When?', 'Where?'.

- Examine the evidence.
- Ask questions.
- Think about the motives of the people providing the information.
- Do not trust the information until you have good cause to do so.

### Who is providing the information?

As we know, anyone can set up a website, so can you find out who has written the information and who has published it? You need to decide if they are trust-worthy, or are trying to persuade you, sell you something, inform or misinform you? You can get some clues by looking for:

- the author's name;
- the organisation publishing the information;
- the contact information;
- the 'about us' pages;
- the URL.

URL stands for Uniform Resource Locator and is the web address of the page you are accessing. They look something like this: http://www.rdn.ac.uk/news/index.html. URLs may look difficult to unravel, but the best way to work out 'who' and 'where' is to break down the URL into its component parts. Table 3.1 shows how to break down the web address.

The organisation code can tell you about who owns the site:

- ac. = academic community servers (that is, universities and colleges);
- edu. = educational and is used in the United States;
- co. or com. = commercial servers;
- gov. = government servers;
- org. = non-governmental, non-profit-making organisations.

Country codes also give us clues as to the origin of the site, although not all URLs include them. For example, au. is Australia, ca. is Canada, de. is Germany and uk. is United Kingdom.

- The site may be provided by an official organisation, or an author who might list qualifications. You can check these if you do not recognise them. But be careful – organisations sometimes sell web page space and they may have little control over the content.
- There are also many pages written by amateurs; some are very good but they do need treating with caution.
- Commercial companies want to sell things, it will be unlikely that you will get unbiased information.

**TABLE 3.1** How to unravel a URL (Source: adapted from www.bbc.co.uk/webwise)

| URL | What's this? | Tell me more... |
|---|---|---|
| http:// | Transfer protocol | The first part of the URL is called the protocol. It tells your browser how to deal with the file that it is about to open. The most common you will see is http, or hypertext transfer protocol. |
| www.rdn | Server name | This refers to the computer (or server) where the web pages or files you want to view are located. It usually contains the name of the organisation responsible for the site; in this case, 'rdn' (the resource discovery network). |
| ac | Top-level domain/ organisational code | This tells you something about the type of organisation responsible for the site (see above for more information). |
| uk | Country code | This tells you in which country the site is located (find out more above). |
| news | Directory | This is a specific folder of information on the server (although it is not always given). There can be any number of these in a URL, indicated by '/' characters. |
| index.html | File name / file type | This is the file you are, or will be, viewing. In this case, html (hypertext mark-up language) is the language of the world wide web. This can change depending on the type of file, e.g. '.mov' is a video file; '.doc' is a document; '.gif' is an image. |

- Government departments and other political organisations are likely to favour information that promotes their political aims.
- Technical information may have been presented in a simple form for the general public or it may be for specialists and assumes you have prior knowledge of the subject.

### When was the information written?

We assume the web is up to date, but there may be a time delay in updating or adding information. Some information is out of date; some sites have just been abandoned; and some sites change or disappear without warning. Reliable sites usually tell you when they were updated.

Ask yourself:

- when the information was originally produced;
- if it is still being preserved in its original form;
- if it is still useful;
- it has been updated;
- if it is going to be updated; and
- if you can find a publication date?

If you are looking for older information, and it is in printed form, it might make sense to ask your librarian to help you, or you could contact the publisher or author.

### Where is the information coming from?

Information on the internet might be located on a computer anywhere in the world, so where it originates may affect the way the information is presented. Look at the URL or the 'About Us' section to see if it can tell you where a site is based.

Academic and government sites may offer some guarantee of quality (ac. or gov.). Non-profit organisations (.org) and commercial companies (.co) or (.com) are not regulated externally, so the quality of the information depends on the reliability of the company or organisation. Internet resources change constantly. A site that moves or changes its layout a lot may not be particularly reliable or useful. Even the most established sites may change their address occasionally. If this happens, a link to the new address is usually provided. If a favourite website suddenly disappears, try looking for its name on a search engine.

## Downloadable articles and books

As you have seen, many organisations and government sites on the internet offer access to texts such as journals, newspaper articles, conference papers, study tips and so on. But there is considerable variation in what they offer:

- Some are published in print, others are only on the web.
- Some can be downloaded free of charge.
- Some provide a 'read-only' text (this cannot be printed).
- Some are in PDF (portable document format), which does not permit changes to the text.
- Some you can only see the title and an abstract, and you have to take out a subscription.

How easily you can download texts will depend on what your learning resources centre subscribes to. For some you need a username password such as an Athens account. This is an access management system that provides users with a single sign-on to numerous websites. Others you may only be able to access through your learning resources centre's intranet and will need your student ID. A few provide open access to all. Some useful sites have been provided at the end of this chapter.

## Choosing the best source for your information

Perhaps the first question you will have to ask yourself when you start to support your own work is, 'What will be the best way to find the information I need?' In many cases it will be the internet, but this does not necessarily have the answer to every question. Let us therefore think about other sources.

- If you want to get answers quickly and correctly, sometimes there is no point in using the internet; you might find it takes twice as long to get half the information you could have got elsewhere.
- If the book is on a shelf in the LRC, why not use it?
- If you do not have immediate access to the book(s) you need, the internet may well be the fastest way of obtaining the information you require.
- If you need to manipulate the data once you have found it, it is easier to download data from the internet rather than copying tables or charts from a book.
- If you want to find companies or businesses, you might find it easier to use the Yellow Pages search engine (http://search.yell.com).
- Do you need an overview of a subject or in-depth information? Some search engines, such as Yahoo!, will provide you with a good overview of sites that cover your area of interest, while others, such as 'Ask Jeeves', will provide you with answers to your question and suggest background reading.
- Do you really understand the information you have been asked to provide? In this case an index/directory-based search engine such as www.rdn.ac.uk, which will explain terms and definitions, can be used if you don't know the most appropriate ones to use.
- Does the information need to be up to date? If so, you will need to check the date of printed texts or books.
- Do you need to be absolutely certain of your answer? You need to be wary of the internet as there is no checking procedure.
- Do you need an international perspective? The internet scores very highly here.

# ■ Reading effectively

So now you have found some texts, either in your learning resources centre or on the internet, how can you find out quickly how useful they are? We read in different ways to suit different purposes. Reading a novel is completely different from reading the newspaper or finding out what is on at the cinema. The way we read is determined by how important we think the text is. This is why we quite often find it difficult to read academic texts in a relaxed way; yet you will absorb more information if you are relaxed. So always make sure the lighting is right for you, you are warm enough, there are no distractions and you have water to hand. Remind yourself of the tips for creating a good study environment in Chapter 1.

Research indicates that we are much less efficient at reading text on screen. Wherever possible, it makes sense to print out what you can. You will then have the text to hand whenever you want it, and can use your travelling time to read it.

## Scanning, skimming and other short cuts

You could read all the texts you have found word by word, but that would take a lot of time. As a general rule you should only read the whole text without checking to see if it is useful first if:

- it is a set text;
- it comes highly recommended by someone whose opinion you value;
- it is the only text you have found; or
- it is so good you can't stop!

Otherwise you will want to check before you start serious reading of a text. Here are some ideas to help speed the process.

- Read the publisher's 'blurb'; often this is on the inside or on the back.
- Look at the introduction to see if it is the right approach for you.
- Scan the contents page, just like you would look for a number in a telephone directory. Do the entries appear to cover the topic? Is it at the right level for you?
- Are there diagrams, examples or illustrations that look useful?
- Look up some of your keywords in the index and then read through a few of the pages they refer to. Does the author deal with the topic in a way that will be useful for you?
- Scan the article for your keywords. Read the sentence that contains one. Does it look useful?
- Read the conclusions.

Jamil suggests that you 'Put your texts into order as soon as you get them. Highlight and learn to skim-read.'

If you have found things that look as if they might be useful, mark them in some way:

- Use markers that are labelled or colour coded.
- If the text is printed from the internet, or you own the book, use a highlighter and put notes in the margin.
- Keep a list of useful pages attached to the book or text.
- Keep postcards or a notebook handy. Note all the details about the article or book to help find valuable pages when you want them.

You will need to record bibliographic details so that you can retrieve what you have found at a later date. These are: author, date of publication; title of article; title of book or journal; publisher and place of publication if it is a book; volume and/or issue number for articles in papers and journals; and page numbers with a small note about the topic.

You can photocopy the really useful pages if there are only a few. This saves carrying too many books. If you are photocopying, always make sure you write all the bibliographic information on the copy; it is very frustrating when you want to use the information at a later date and you cannot find it again. Even if you have a lot to read, it still makes sense to skim-read. A lot of people use skimming to help them identify useful information quickly, or to gain an overview before reading a text in detail. There are different ways to do this; you will develop your own with practice. An example is:

- read the title, sub-headings and summaries;
- study the diagrams, illustrations, tables or charts;
- read the first and last paragraphs to see what the article or chapter is about;
- read the first sentence of each paragraph;
- if it seemed interesting, let your eyes skim over text at about three times the speed you usually read and take in the keywords and the general gist;
- keep thinking about the meaning of what you are reading.

**ACTIVITY**

Skim an article in a newspaper or journal. Put it to one side and make a list. What was it about? What were the key points? Now read it again very carefully. How much did you find out? How much was missing? Hopefully, you were surprised at how much you had identified.

## Reflective and critical reading

You will need to vary your reading speed depending on how difficult the text is to understand. Be clear about what you want to find out when you start. Have a dictionary, technical guide or an internet-linked computer to hand, so if you find words you don't understand you can look them up. It is useful to keep a list of new words with their definitions in your notebook. Don't worry if you are a bit slow to start with; reading with understanding improves the more you do it. If a text is difficult, read it fairly quickly, then read it again more slowly.

**ACTIVITY**

Practise reading a newspaper article for two minutes. How much did you read? Did you understand what you were reading? Repeat this activity using different texts. Try to get your reading speed up to 200 words a minute, but remember it is more important to understand what you read than to read quickly.

## ■ Making notes

There are two types of note making that you will encounter in your studies. These are:

- making notes from your reading and other research; and
- making notes in taught sessions.

There are many different ways to make notes; what is important is that you choose a method that enables you to find your notes easily and understand them at a later stage. Different methods may be useful at different times.

**ACTIVITY**

Read a passage or study a diagram, and then close the book. Without looking at it again write or draw the key points. Read the rest of this chapter and then look back at your notes of the key points. Does it make any sense to you or do you need to change your way of making notes?

### Ways of making notes from texts

*Notes on handouts/books*

Although it is quick and useful to write notes on texts when you are skimming and scanning at the first stage, the notes are often difficult to understand later. You will probably end up having to read it all over again. Always start by heading the notes with the bibliographic details, including pages, or volume, issue and page numbers for journals or articles. Leave spaces so you can fill things in later. Number your pages and put a brief title on each.

## Summary notes

This involves reading all the text and rewriting a summary of each paragraph or section in your own words. The advantage of this method is that it helps you to practise writing and thinking. The disadvantage is that it is slow, and written notes are not always easy to revise from if you are a visual learner, as the key points do not stand out.

## Headings with bullet points

This method is particularly useful if you are working straight onto the computer. The heading is the key point or question and the bullets are all the points that come within that heading. Although it can be quite difficult at first, it does make you think more carefully about what you are reading and is easy to revise from or use later.

## 'Mind maps' or 'sprays'

These involve identifying the key point or question, placing it in the middle of a page and drawing from it lines with themes written along them. Each line leads you into greater depth and may sub-divide each time you find another related point. These can be coloured to make points stand out. They can allow you to summarise many pages of reading and you concentrate on identifying the themes. They can be fun and stimulating to do because they are different and visual, but they can be too superficial for complex ideas and quite difficult to revise from. If you are interested in this technique, look at Tony Buzan's (1970) mind-mapping book. Caroline tells us, 'My learning style is visual, so coloured mind maps really work for me'.

## Linear notes

This method involves identifying key points and ideas, using your own style and developing a personal shorthand. It makes you think clearly, builds on methods you are already familiar with and can be quite easy to revise from. It is a good idea to use dotted lines, boxes, arrows, highlighting or other visual markers to make things stand out; or you could turn information into tables, charts or numbered lists. It is a bad idea to copy text unless you can see that it would make an excellent quotation. If you decide to do this, make sure you identify the page number as well as all the bibliographic data you have. Write down things to remember, for example 'good diagram p.149'.

Do not waste time writing too much or rewriting notes; it is better to go over them and use markers to make them clearer for you. Bob says:

> 'I cannot stress enough the need to work through all the set reading. Finish it daily; don't let it pile up. Highlight important information and write your own summary – that's the best way of remembering things.'

Dom advises, 'Keep your notes safe in special folders; they are very important for the course'.

## Taking notes in lectures and classes

Making notes in taught sessions can be useful to help you concentrate, to make things clearer and to help you remember what has been said. They are also excellent for revision.

Most courses have handbooks and session outlines, so, wherever possible, do use the recommended reading or research to prepare. Christina advises you to 'Take time, time and more time. Have a separate notebook for each module and highlight important facts. Learn to speed-read effectively.'

The fine details of most sessions should be available as handouts, web pages or recommended reading. So you do not need to write everything down, but you do need to have notes, which will help you understand the handouts at a later date.

- Put the title, date and name of the lecturer on your notes; it will help with storage and retrieval of information at a later date.
- Listen carefully to the introduction. This is where key themes are usually identified. Make a note of them.
- Recognise the way key points are identified. Listen for signal words such as 'firstly', 'secondly', 'most importantly', 'in addition', 'on the other hand', 'for example'.
- Summarise what is being said in your own words. Most often, key points are repeated in slightly different words. This will give you some extra writing time.
- If you miss a point, star the space and make a note to look at the handouts to fill this in.
- Listen to the summary carefully; this will also help you to organise your notes and fill in any missing information.

- Ask questions at the end if you do not understand. Do not think that this will make you look silly. More often than not you will ask a question that others will have wanted to ask.
- Do not do things that will distract you, e.g. doodling, looking out of the window or fidgeting; these diminish concentration.
- Avoid jumping to conclusions or making hasty judgements; negativity and bias can get in the way of listening.
- After the lecture, mark up, underline, star or use other ways that work for you to identify important facts, dates and things that are new to you and need following up.
- Review your notes regularly. In this way you will become familiar with them and will also know where to find them.

A useful tip is to go over notes with fellow students. Check your understanding with each other. Support groups are invaluable, especially if studying at this level is new to you.

## Keeping your information accessible and safe

How you organise and store your information is extremely important. Many hours can be wasted looking for something you dimly remember as being important. This is personal and you should develop your technique to suit yourself. However, it is worthwhile considering the following points.

- Transfer the material you have gained from lectures, reading, data gathering and so on into your storage system as soon as possible.
- If you transfer most of your work to the computer, make sure you have copies on a disk or memory stick and have printed off hard copies for the day when you have a power cut.
- Keep your notes for each course or module together in a logical sequence, in a separate notebook or file. You should be able to take this with you to the next taught session, the tutorial or the learning resources centre with ease.
- Use file dividers and label them and your files clearly.
- Keep an up-to-date contents page.
- Create a bibliography and make notes to tell you which topic they are useful for.

This chapter has probably given you a great deal to think about. We do not expect you to be able to absorb it all at once. Dip into it from time to time to remind yourself of the points covered. On the other hand you will recognise most of them as common sense. If you adhere to them they should help you to enjoy your time of study.

## ■ Websites to visit for more information

www.bbc.co.uk/webwise/learn – the BBC's free course guide to using the internet.

www.blackwellpublishing.com/sociolog/res.asp – this will give you access to any OPAC in the UK. It is the publishing index to sociology resources.

www.imperial.ac.uk/educationaldevelopment/e-learning/learningtolearn.htm – go to this site for downloadable Learning to Learn.

www.mindtools.com/rdstratg.html – for strategies to help you read more quickly and effectively.

www.rdn.ac.uk – the Resource Discovery Network will give you on-line tutorial support in finding useful texts and electronic links to directories, gateways, databases, library catalogues and so on. Tutorial support can be found through www.rdn.ac.uk, then click on virtual training suite, then social science research methods.

www.wiltscoll.ac.uk/learning/study_skills/research_skills_3.asp – this is an excellent site for hints on searching for information.

## ■ Electronic journals

These journals and magazines give free access to all:
www.blackwellpublishing.com – *Higher Education Quarterly*.
www.tandf.co.uk/journals/carfax – includes the *British Educational Research Journal*.
http://ioewebserver.ioe.ac.uk/ioe/cms/get.asp?cid=9634 – the Institute of Education Library's e-journal listing.

## ■ References

Buzan, T. (1970) *The Mind Map Book: How to Use Radiant Thinking to Maximize Your Brain's Untapped Potential*. New York: Penguin.
www.bbc.co.uk/webwise/learn – BBC webwise.

# 4 Developing your oral presentation skills

## Why make presentations?

We all know that making presentations is one of the greatest causes of anxiety. Few can actually say they enjoy the process. So why do your tutors insist that you should make them? In the last chapter we investigated ways of finding information, recording it and storing it, but, of course, it's not a lot of use to you just filed away. Knowing how to present your learning is a really useful skill. You will be surprised how many times you might be called on during your career to make a presentation in a more formal situation. You may be asked to make a short presentation about an aspect of a job you are being interviewed for, or you could at a later date be making a presentation of your work at a conference, or trying to persuade clients. So, the more you participate in seminars and tutorials the better. Getting used to speaking in front of people is a good way to prepare you for making presentations. Oral communication cannot be taught; this chapter can only show you the way, so the more you practise, the better.

Presentations are a particularly good way to consolidate your learning about a topic, because you have to think carefully about the content and approach. Researching and learning about a topic in preparation for making a presentation often makes it easier to remember the information. Presentations also show to others what you know and understand. For instance, your presentation could be a very good way for your tutor to make an assessment of what you know. It can also help to make the subject clearer for your fellow students. For some students a presentation may allow them to show a wider range of skills, particularly if they feel they are better at talking than writing. Quite often you will be given a choice of topic and you will be presenting something that interests you.

There are different types of presentation that you might be asked to make, and for different reasons. Your presentation will most likely be 10 to 15 minutes long followed by a discussion. Usually only very experienced presenters are asked to talk for more than 20 minutes. Broadly speaking, the presentations you make will form part of your assessment process, but some may not. Those that do may be assessed formally by your tutor and allocated a grade or mark, or assessed informally. In both cases you will most likely be given verbal or written feedback on your performance. Sometimes your peers will assess your presentation. This can also be very helpful as it will give you useful clues for improving your skills. You might also make informal presentations where you are not assessed. However, wherever possible, ask for feedback, because it always helps to know how effective you were.

You may be asked to give a group presentation or to be part of a series of presentations. This is one of the ways that tutors allocate the responsibility of sharing knowledge and making a session more memorable. Group presentations are also an excellent way for you to learn to work closely with colleagues.

You may be asked to give a poster presentation. This is usually a visual display of the topic you are presenting, which you are prepared to answer questions about or to explain to a small audience. It is a good way to help you understand your subject matter as you will need to be able to synthesise what you know into key points, diagrams, photographs or other visual forms in a sequence.

You may be asked to demonstrate or explain a process or product, such as showing how to prepare a recipe or diagnose a fault in a machine. Although there are some key differences in that you are more likely to be using objects rather than visual representations of them in a demonstration, the key points in this chapter also apply.

## ■ What makes a good presentation?

One way to decide what makes a good presentation is to ask yourself about your past experiences. Always listen carefully to presentations; as well as learning, it will make you a useful critic and will give you further clues about making improvements.

**ACTIVITY**

Think of presentations you have attended. These may vary from a lecture given by a teacher you knew to a presentation made in a public meeting or an address given by one of your peers. Make a list of any good points, and then, in a second column, list the really poor points. Keep this list to hand; it will be useful when you are reading this chapter. You may have identified points that are not mentioned. It is important for you to make sure you remember them also.

## Pre-preparation

The importance of adequate preparation cannot be overstated, but before you start you should know:

- who you are presenting to;
- what your topic is;
- how long you are expected to speak;
- when your presentation is scheduled;
- where the presentation is taking place;
- what audio-visual aids or facilities are available in the presentation room; and
- whether you are expected to provide additional information, such as hand-outs.

Let us look at these points in greater detail.

### To whom are you presenting?

The sort of presentation you will want to make will depend a great deal on your audience. Clearly, fellow students who are not familiar with your topic are not going to require the same depth and volume of information as, for instance, examiners who are very familiar with the topic and are assessing your knowledge. Are there any cultural characteristics you will have to be sensitive towards? Are there members of your audience who speak English as an additional language? Are there health and safety issues you should be familiar with?

### What is your topic?

Are you familiar with the subject matter of the topic you are presenting and are you expected to demonstrate your knowledge, or has the subject been given to you in order that you can polish up and show your research skills, or indeed your presentation skills? Again, the answer to the question will determine the way in which you gather information and make your presentation.

### For how long are you expected to speak?

How long is your talk? It is very important that you know for how long you are allowed or expected, to speak so that you build that into your planning. It is very frustrating to spend a long time preparing a presentation of which you are really proud, only to be stopped before you have finished because you have exceeded your time limit. Further on in the chapter there are some hints to help you get the timing right.

*When is your presentation scheduled for?*

This may seem a silly question but all your hard work will go to waste if you have not noted down the correct time and date. Another good reason for knowing the time is that the receptiveness of your audience can vary according to the time of day. Think how you feel first thing in the morning and compare it with how attentive you are immediately after lunch. Some people feel very sleepy after lunch so you may need to consider taking a more lively approach.

*Where is the presentation taking place?*

Are you following on from someone else, or will you need to make sure the room is available and ready? Hopefully, this is not something you should have to worry about, but it is well worth checking because it will put your mind at rest and allow you to concentrate on making the presentation successful.

*What audio-visual aids or facilities are available to you in the presentation room?*

Always check what audio-visual aids are available, and whose responsibility it is for ensuring everything will be there for you before you start planning. Do you want to show a video? Is there a player to hand or do you have to order one? If so, how? Can you ask your tutor to get one for you? Does the room have darkening facilities of some sort? Will your audience be able to see the screen? What about PowerPoint? Is your disk, memory stick, laptop, or whatever you have the information on compatible with the hardware in the room? Your tutor or whoever is responsible for audio-visual aids should be able to help you check. It is essential that you get answers to these questions, as it will determine the way in which you can make your presentation.

*Are you expected to provide additional information such as handouts?*

In some cases you will be expected to provide handouts such as copies of your presentation. Maybe you want your audience to look at photographs, texts, diagrams etc., which cannot be put on a screen. Check if reproduction facilities are available for your use; also check how large your audience will be and estimate how many copies you will need.

## Preparation

Once you know all the answers to the pre-preparation questions, you can really concentrate on preparing what you are going to say and how. Remember there are Five Rs for preparation to be effective:

- research the topic;

- review the data;
- read it out loud;
- rehearse reading the presentation and using the visual aids;
- [be] ready to present.

## Research the topic

Researching the topic that you are going to present is essential. With your mind firmly on the topic – whether it was your choice or not makes no difference – ask yourself the following questions:

- What does my audience need to know?
- What is the main argument?
- What are the key points I want to make?
- What is my conclusion?

Imagine you are in the audience; think of all the questions you would want answers to on your topic. Ask your friends, family and colleagues what questions they would ask. Make a note of them and organise them in order of importance and sense. Then find the answers to the questions. Now you should have all the information you need for your presentation. Much of the information should be in those carefully organised notes you have taken at recent seminars or in reading around your subject, which was covered in the last chapter. If on the other hand you have been asked to prepare something you know very little about, you will most often have been given some clues about where to start. If not, the previous chapter should have given you some useful hints on where to find information. Once you have collected together all that you think you will need, make a rough plan. You will find some guidance about planning in the section on essay writing in Chapter 6.

With your plan of points beside you, write the presentation out in rough, considering at the same time how you can turn some of your points into visual data.

The structure of your presentation should be like this:

- a title that gives a good idea what the presentation is about;
- the introduction, which will identify what you are covering and will describe, briefly, how it is structured;
- the main body of the presentation where you expand on the points you identified in the introduction, either sequentially or in order of interest, with the best first; and
- the conclusion, a summary of the key points you have made.

The advantage of structuring your presentation in this way is that putting the most interesting points first means that if you do run short of time you have said the most important things, so it is not too much of a problem. Additionally, it can stimulate more questions at the end, because your audience know from the start what you are aiming at. It is also easier for you to find where you are if you temporarily lose your place.

## Review the data

Review the information you have gathered together.

- Read your script; is there anything that is not needed? Cut out unnecessary information, even though you think it might be interesting, if it does not fit into the time allowed.
- Is there anything you have included that you do not really understand? You have three options here: either read around it; get clarification of it; or delete it.
- How are you going to present the information? There are a number of different options available to you.

You could make your presentation with one or more of the following more commonly used visual presentation techniques:

### Handouts

Advantages:

- they give your audience a means of preparing for your talk;
- they can be referred to by the speaker to amplify a point;
- they provide a means of giving visual data such as photographs;
- they give your audience a means of checking what they have missed.

Disadvantages:

- the audience is reading and may therefore not be listening carefully;
- rustling papers can be distracting for the speaker and for those listening;
- unless they add to the presenter's points the audience may feel cheated; they may as well just take their own notes.

### Overhead transparencies

Advantages:

- easy and flexible to use – you can write on them at the time;
- easy to produce – most photocopiers can reproduce them;
- coloured reproductions look good;
- total darkness is not needed.

Disadvantages:

- they can be of poor quality;
- they tend to be seen as inferior to PowerPoint;
- colour can be expensive to produce.

### PowerPoint

Advantages:

- looks professional and is easy to use after some instruction;
- can use a combination of text, diagrams and visuals;
- can show text in different ways, introducing each point in turn.

Disadvantages:

- it is becoming too commonplace;
- compatibility of data source and projector must be checked beforehand – always have an alternative available, transparencies for instance; technology can let you down;
- gimmicks, such a sound effects, flying text etc., can be annoying.

### Flipcharts or whiteboard

Advantages:

- excellent for interactive presentations;
- key points from discussions can be recorded visually;
- you can prepare in advance;
- easy to make visual points, which can be added to while talking.

Disadvantages:

- you need to practise writing and drawing with confidence and clarity;
- can be seen as amateur;
- not suitable for a large audience or a large auditorium.

### Photographic slides

Advantages:

- good for quality, especially art works or historical data;
- not commonplace;
- easy to manage.

Disadvantages:

- quality can be lost when transferring to another medium such as printing or PowerPoint;
- can be seen as old-fashioned;
- slides can often end up upside-down or back-to-front;
- not good for text;
- need a darkened room.

### Film, video or DVD

Advantages:

- help audience become situated in the presentation more easily;
- readily available in large numbers and extracts may be excellent to illustrate a point;
- easy to produce yourself.

Disadvantages:

- can be soporific (send audience to sleep) especially in the after-lunch period;
- need a darkened room;
- technology must be compatible.

You could make your presentation without any visual aids. This may be easier to prepare and manage; indeed, some really accomplished presenters need nothing more. However, it is worth considering that visual information helps your audience to concentrate on what you are saying and makes it more interesting for them. Your audience may also contain learners who find it easier to take in information visually. Most importantly, visual aids can help *you* remember what you are going to say next!

## Read your presentation out loud

Now you have the draft of your presentation, you have pruned all the unnecessary parts and you have prepared the plans for your visuals, it is time for a first run-through. Read your text out loud and practise moving at the same time. Will you be placing transparencies onto the projector or operating the computer? Keep your eye on the clock. Time yourself. Remember, you will need to speak more slowly than your normal talking speed; between 130 and 160 words per minute is recommended when presenting; this will enable your audience to understand what you are saying and to take notes if they want to. Take a moment to breathe between each point.

Check the time. Did you take more or less than the amount of time you have been allocated? Most people prepare far too much. What can you remove to make your talk fit into the time available?

---

**ACTIVITY**

Ask a friend to listen to you critically.

- Take a newspaper article and read it at the pace you think is right for a presentation lasting five minutes.
- Ask if the words were clear and easy to understand.
- Ask if you managed to get expression into your voice.
- Check how many words you read; this will give you a good guide as to how many your presentation should contain.

---

Once you have read through your presentation, it is time to prepare the visual aids. It is worth bearing in mind the following points.

- Use technology as a tool to enhance your talk; it is not a gimmick to impress your tutor and/or colleagues;
- Keep it simple; the more hardware you use the more confusing it is for the audience and the more that can go wrong.
- Visuals should be clear and easy to understand. Use the '6+6+6' rule for PowerPoint slides or for acetates – no more than six words to a line, no more than six lines to a slide and no more then six slides for a ten-minute presentation. As a general rule, allow about two minutes per slide; slightly longer if you are developing more specific points.
- Your audience should be able to understand the visual in about thirty seconds. Check the understanding with someone who has not seen your visual before by getting them to look at it while you talk, and then switching off and asking a few questions that you would want them to have learned.
- Use a good size font that enlarges well – 18 point is the minimum, Arial or Times New Roman. As a general rule you should be able to read the screen with ease from the back of the room you will be presenting in. If you do not know the size of the room, assume a maximum of 15 metres, or check that you can read the acetate from about two metres without projection.
- Colour is interesting, but yellow and orange have a very short focal length and are difficult to see from a distance.

- As a general rule, if you are having text only, white on a blue background or black on a pale background are easier on the eye because the text is clearer to read.
- Avoid using pre-prepared technical or mathematical diagrams, such as you find in textbooks and manuals; they do not project well and are often very difficult to read.
- Check your visuals for spelling and sense. A fresh pair of eyes can usually spot mistakes more easily.

## Rehearse presenting and using the visual aids

Rehearse, rehearse, rehearse! Wafeeq suggests, 'Write your presentation at least one week before the due date. Practise beforehand and then do the final adjustments and editing before your final practice the day before the presentation.' Vasiliki suggests that you should 'plan enough time to complete your work; it always takes longer than you'd expect. Practise presenting it beforehand and then time yourself.' Julie advises:

> 'Don't practise in front of your family!
> The kids rolled about laughing and my husband fell asleep!
> Seriously, though, do practise and feel confident about what you
> are presenting. It is your 15 minutes of fame. If you can get
> access to an interactive whiteboard try out your presentation on
> it, then you get to know how best to use it. I also found that
> having a table nearby was useful so that I could place my
> notes on it rather than hold lots of papers
> in very shaky hands.'

The more familiar you become with your presentation, the more confident you will feel and the easier it will be not to be dependent on the script. Try it out on your own to begin with, then with an audience of friends or colleagues. No matter how nervous you are, it is not a good idea to have the presentation written out like a script for you to read. Try not to learn your text by heart; you will end up reciting it and sounding very boring. Accept that each time you try the presentation out you may use a slightly different grouping of words; this means you have become so familiar with the subject that you can talk with ease. You should know most of what you want to say; it is, however, a good idea to have a prompt sheet. You will, in the end, devise your own method, but here are three suggestions:

- Simplify the text of your presentation; print it at a minimum size of 14-point Arial or Times New Roman. Highlight or embolden the key points of each paragraph. Then, if you glance down, you will be able to pick out where you are quite quickly, even if the light is low.
- Prepare cue cards, which have key words or phrases on them written clearly. Always number cards or pages or attach them together with a treasury tag in case you drop them. Also mark on them which acetate, slide or new PowerPoint page should be on show.
- The text you put on the acetate or screen can act as a prompt as well, so make sure you know how to expand the points you are showing visually.

Be prepared for the worst-case scenario when the technology lets you down and you cannot use the visual aids you have lovingly prepared. Have a back-up plan.

## Ready to present

So now you are ready. The great day has arrived. You have rehearsed, you have taken advice from everyone and everything has been prepared.

Checklist:

- Handouts have been photocopied and you have the correct number.
- Cue cards or highlighted text is in a separate folder, which you can find with ease.
- Visuals are stored on a disk, memory stick, laptop or, in the case of acetates, interleaved with clean paper between each so that you can read what they say.
- You have a back-up plan – perhaps printed copies of the visuals, which can be shared – in case technology lets you down at the last minute.
- You have pens, pencils, flip chart etc. organised as appropriate.
- You have checked the room in advance – even if you are visiting a new venue, you can always go to the room a few hours beforehand to check the technology and make sure everything is in place. Seek help immediately if it is not; technicians are usually available in these situations.
- When checking the room, look for potential problems, such as an overhead projector on one side of the room and the computer and data projector on the other. This type of situation can be the cause of much disturbance and spoil your presentation, not to mention raising a number of health and safety issues. You will have to be prepared to make changes even at this late stage.
- Know where the light switches are so that they can be dimmed easily when needed.

## ■ The presentation

Dress appropriately; your appearance communicates a lot about you before you open your mouth, and first impressions can make a big difference to the way your audience responds to you. The general rule is that you should be neater than average, but not over-dressed. Even if you are making a demonstration, you should ensure that your overall or uniform, for instance, is clean; it shows respect for your audience and shows that you care.

Numerous books and lectures focus on body language; essentially they state that your body expresses attitude and thoughts through its movements. The way you stand will tell your audience what you think of them and the subject, so if you lounge against the wall or a machine, for instance, you will communicate disinterest in both. Similarly, how you speak is as important as what you say. No matter how nervous you are feeling, you are in control. Speak clearly and, if you value the advice of voice coaches, in a slightly deeper voice than usual. You will already have practised using the correct speed, and try to avoid using slang or colloquialisms; only use terms you know your audience will understand or those you want them to learn. Marisa suggests that in the few minutes before you start presenting you try '747' breathing to calm your nerves: 'Breathe in for a count of 7, out for 4 and then in for 7; it really works', while Christina advises that, 'It can be a daunting experience and nerves can take over. Just remember everyone's in the same boat and that you've practised beforehand, many times.'

Remember, it is hard for your audience to listen attentively the whole time; attention is generally very good to begin with, gradually declining towards the middle and then improving towards the end. As we noted before, the level of concentration will vary according to a number of factors such as the time of day and, perhaps, what your audience has been engaged in immediately prior to your presentation.

Greet your audience. What you say will vary according to the type of presentation you are making. If you are not well known to your audience say, for example, 'good morning' and tell them who you are. Do not apologise for things you have not done. Then you let your audience know what you are going to tell them; this way they know what to expect. Imagine they are asking, 'Why should I listen to this?' If you have not told them you will lose their attention; so try to make it as interesting as possible.

Keep to the time you have been allocated; don't be tempted to stray from your original plan or you could use up useful time that you have not planned in. Try to speak clearly, pitching your voice to the back of the room; this will help your voice carry. No matter how nervous you are, you will be forgiven if your presentation is clear and engaging. Be natural but not too friendly, try to vary your voice, look at your audience but don't fix on a particular person or it will make them feel uncomfortable. Pause at the key points, this helps to emphasise them and will give you a chance to glance at your prompts.

Unless you know that you are good at telling jokes don't be tempted, they can be disastrous. Try to stand in a position where you do not obscure the screen.

Use your hands, but not too much. Also try to avoid pacing up and down; it is very distracting, although some movement is a good idea. Have some water to hand; it is amazing how dry nerves can cause you to become. Smile and enjoy; your audience want you to succeed. Whatever you do, no matter how nervous you are; DO NOT read the visuals to your audience; at best it is boring and at worst it implies that your audience is incapable of reading for themselves.

Finally, watch your audience's body language; it may make sense for you to cut part of the presentation and draw the conclusions. Leave enough time for questions and have one prepared to ask them if none are forthcoming. This will help to stimulate discussion, which will give you very useful feedback on your presentation. Virginia reminds us that 'we are all here to learn and improve'.

## Answering the questions

This is often the part of a presentation that the presenter most fears. Your thorough preparation will ensure you know your data. Tell yourself that. The rest is common sense and remaining calm. Additionally, it is better to have stimulated your audience to want to ask questions than for there to be a stunned silence when you finish. Questions are an excellent way for you to gauge how clear you were in expressing your ideas, how pertinent or topical they were, and to give you the opportunity to expand on points, showing yet more of your knowledge. It is also an excellent way for you to learn other viewpoints on the subject or gain additional insights.

So in what form might those questions come? Some questioners are:

- seeking for additional information or clarification;
- wanting to show you how much they know;
- holding an opposing viewpoint;
- wanting you to agree with their viewpoint and they won't give up until you do;
- wanting to use the opportunity to make a public statement about something that often has nothing to do with your topic.

As a new presenter you are unlikely to have to deal with all the categories of questioner until you start to present in more public places such as conferences. However, it would make sense to think about the best way to deal with questions.

**ACTIVITY**

Think how you would handle the following questions:

- Could you expand on your point about . . . ?
- I really cannot agree with your point about . . .
- Have you come across the work of . . . who is an expert in this field?

- I still don't think you have answered my question.
- What is your source for claiming...?

Can you think of other questions that might come your way?

## Group presentations

The benefits of group presentations are that, firstly, all the points we have considered are shared and, secondly, that you learn from collaboration. The disadvantages are that you may not necessarily agree on how the presentation should take place or the content, or indeed how to share the preparation. Additionally, when you share responsibility there is more opportunity for overlooking organisational details.

So make sure you:

- build in enough joint planning time;
- all understand and are agreed on what each of you are responsible for preparing;
- are all familiar with the shape of the presentation;
- have all discussed and agreed the content;
- all know your roles for the actual presentation;
- have contingency plans agreed between you if a member of the group does not arrive.

If you are being assessed as a team, try to ensure the jobs are divided evenly. Resentment created by all team members achieving a communal mark for different levels of input can be harmful to further collaboration.

Learning by making a presentation is another way for you to gain knowledge about your subject. The more you make yourself take part in seminars and discussions and take opportunities to make presentations, the more you will increase your learning. Additionally, you will have honed and polished a skill, which will have so many applications in your future. Very few of us are natural performers; most of us have developed our own techniques over the years. It may also interest you to know that many public performers feel anxious and more than a little nervous each time they present themselves. In fact, they consider that this helps them to sharpen their performance and shows that they have respect for their craft and for their audience.

## Recommended reading

Microsoft Step-by-Step (2003) *PowerPoint 2003 On-Line-Training Solutions.* Redmond, WA: Microsoft.

# 5 Data collection and presentation

## Why collect data?

It is almost certain that you will be expected to collect and analyse data during the process of completing your foundation degree. Collecting data is one of the oldest and certainly most widely used ways in which we find out about things we want to know. Other terms we use, such as research, investigation, enquiry and study, are all used in this chapter. This may seem confusing, particularly as the word research is often associated with highly intelligent people or large organisations using rigorous and complicated methods. However, it can be argued that whenever we seek to find answers to a question we are 'doing research'. Bell (1995:2), referring to Howard and Sharpe (1983), claims that research is, 'seeking through methodological processes to add to one's body of knowledge and hopefully that of others'.

In Chapter 3 we investigated ways of finding and storing data for your studies; some of the techniques you have learned will be invaluable for what follows. This chapter aims to help you complete enquiry or research tasks. It offers suggestions and reflections on how you can carry out well-planned, methodologically sound and well-written research, and submit it on time. There is a wide range of texts written for researchers ranging from those like you to those engaged in work at post-doctoral level. A few suggestions for further reading have been included at the end of the chapter, together with some useful websites.

However, all the reading in the world will not make you skilled; in fact there is a danger that too much knowledge can make you so indecisive that you never get started. What this chapter will do is alert you to the fact that when you are researching, everything you do must be thought through very carefully in advance before you act. It will offer useful clues on how to help your thinking. By wasting your respondent's time on an ill-conceived survey, for example, relationships may be damaged.

Research is not abstract or complicated; if you look at Chapter 6 you will find it is much like writing an essay; it has a beginning, a middle and an end.

Beginning – planning:

- deciding what to research;
- formulating and clarifying the research topic.

Middle – implementation:

- reviewing the literature;
- choosing the research method;
- negotiating access;
- planning and conducting the research.

End – conclusion:

- analysing the data;
- writing the project report.

The research process is often described as being linear, in that one stage leads to the next, and so on, but experience has shown that, frequently, it is not; one stage often overlaps with another. So, although this chapter has to be written in a linear fashion, try to bear this in mind when you are reading it.

## Different categories of data

Broadly speaking, there are three categories of data:

- primary data, which comes from the source at the time of the event; it may be a report, newspaper article, film footage, or a live or recorded interview;
- secondary data is usually what was written about an event some time afterwards and will include commentaries, compilations and written texts; and
- statistical data, which comes from sources such as a census or survey.

## What type of data collection?

There are two main categories of data collection, quantitative and qualitative:

### Quantitative data collection

For many years this was the preferred way of carrying out research. Quantitative researchers collect facts and study the relationship between one set and another. It is often used to test out theories such as the effectiveness of new drugs on patients in health care, and to gather large amounts of information. Because statistical methods are used to analyse the data, quantitative research is regarded as scientific and providing reliable information. This encourages funders to give considerable financial support. Additionally, quantitative data collection can be a relatively inexpensive way of undertaking market research and gauging public opinion through surveys and questionnaires. Its main weakness is in the methodology itself, because it uses very rigid methods to measure and analyse the information. It is considered by many to be unsuited to measuring human reactions, emotions and attitudes.

### Qualitative data collection

Qualitative research is almost the opposite of quantitative research. Researchers using this type of data collection are more concerned with trying to gain an insight into human perception of the world and, as such, recognise that it is not wise to generalise about human reactions, opinions, attitudes and so on. Additionally, in this method, the hypothesis or theory comes after the data collection. Its advantage is that it allows the researcher to make distinctions between responses, and it reports on everything that is said about a topic.

There are claims from supporters of the scientific approach that the qualitative method is weak because it often uses only quite small amounts of data in comparison with surveys, for example, and therefore its findings cannot be generalised. However, there is a growing understanding among the research communities that so long as the research methods have been used thoroughly the findings from qualitative research are as reliable as those from quantitative methods. The primary disadvantage of qualitative research is that it can be quite expensive to carry out. Over the last few years there has been a growing belief that the two methods complement one another and researchers frequently use both methods.

## Determining what to research

As a beginner you are most likely to be asked to conduct a small-scale research project and qualitative methods will be most appropriate. Therefore, the key focus of this chapter is on introducing the most common methods. This will enable you to select the most suitable way to collect and analyse your data. There will be a brief mention of the types of methods and statistical analysis required for quantitative research, and references, which you can follow up. This will be particularly important for you if, for instance, you are asked to contribute to a larger piece of research and were not involved in its design. You will need to make sure you understand the reasons for its design. This chapter will help you identify the sorts of questions you should be asking the research designer.

### Choosing the topic area

Most often you will be asked to identify your research topic, in some instances you may be given one, in which case the decision is already made for you.

Here are some examples of initial ideas for research:

- the quality of life for newly admitted clients in residential care;
- difficulties experienced by young parents in a new neighbourhood;
- the impact of new road layout for drivers of HGVs;
- the value of assertiveness training for victims of crime;
- successful youth work.

You may have a clear idea already of something you wish to find out, or, more often, there may be several things that seem to be of equal importance. You can only choose one, so making a decision is the first thing you have to do.

To help you make a decision you could:

- check the library catalogue to see if the topic you are interested in has been researched already;
- check the titles of dissertations to see if your topic, or one like it, is there;
- ask your tutor for some advice;
- check with colleagues and fellow students.

**ACTIVITY**

Think of a research topic and using the methods above find similar titles. Make a note of the way you found the most useful information.

## Checking if you can manage the research

### Is it realistic and achievable?

As beginning researchers we often have exciting ideas that are completely unrealistic. This is often because we have not thought through the amount of information our investigation might generate. On the other hand we may not have considered the difficulties of obtaining the data. Perhaps it is confidential and not in the public domain, perhaps it has not been recorded, or it has been recorded in a way that you will not be able to understand easily. You may not have access to the people you need to talk to. There is a whole range of obstacles that could prevent you from being successful in achieving your goal. It is essential that you look at them realistically, and seek help from your tutor or colleagues in looking for solutions or alternatives.

### Do you have a deadline to meet?

Your degree specification and your tutor will be quite clear about the deadlines that you have to meet. Only you can know how quickly you are able to undertake certain tasks. One of the most fundamental tasks you should undertake is to make a timeline. Build in extra time to accommodate those unforeseen obstacles – illness, a family crisis and so on. Put it somewhere visible so that it acts as a permanent reminder. Be ready to make adjustments if you cannot achieve your goals. You may need to negotiate this with your tutor, so don't leave it till the last minute.

### Does it fit within the expectations of the subject you are studying?

Although you may be given some freedom in deciding your topic, it makes no sense at all to research something that is not going to contribute to your knowledge of the subject. Indeed, it is often very difficult to get colleagues or research subjects to co-operate if they cannot see the relevance of a piece of research. On the other hand, you will be surprised at how helpful others can be if they consider the results of your labours will be useful to them.

### Are you interested in the topic?

This is probably the most important question to ask yourself. All research entails a certain amount of drudgery and hard work and you will need a real interest in the subject to help you through the difficult times. However, no matter how interested you are you do have to keep an open mind about the subject and be careful not to pre-judge the answers.

Discuss your proposed area of research with your tutor and agree what the emphasis of your study will be.

## Formulating and clarifying the research topic

You have decided on a general topic area that interests you, you are sure you can manage the timing and you have access to the sorts of data you think you are going to need. Now you have to be absolutely clear about what it is you want to find out. Usually, the easiest way to direct your thinking is to formulate questions that will help to provide you with answers. Think carefully about what is worth investigating, deciding on the aims for your study. Start to think about the way in which you could collect your information. Keep notes at all times and keep them safely together.

For example, as a craftsperson you wish to find out if there are families where someone makes things in their spare time. Before you can start you would need to define some of your terms:

- What do you mean by 'family'? Will any group living together count?
- What do you mean by 'make'? Does repairing or putting kits together count?

- How will you define spare time?
- Do you mean making things as a hobby? What about unemployed people?
- Will you take account of age, gender or ethnicity?
- How will you select your families?

You need to be clear about your terms because you can't change your mind half-way through.

---

**ACTIVITY**

Think of the things you need to know about the following topic before you start to plan the research. Does the distance travelled have any effect on student performance?

---

Should we re-phrase this question to say, 'Is there any relationship between the distance travelled by a student to their place of study and their academic achievement?' What else did you decide? We need some definitions:

- How are we defining student? Will it complicate things if we accept the full age-range?
- What do we mean by 'distance'?
- How are we going to define detrimental? Do we mean they get low marks, or fail to complete work on time?
- Can we get access to this kind of data?
- How else could you get information, which might help to answer the question? You could try asking the students a series of questions. Will that help?

Finding answers to the following questions before talking to your tutor again will be helpful:

- What is your topic area?
- What do you want to find out?
- Which kinds of questions will provide you with the most accurate data?
- How will you collect the data?
- How will it be analysed?
- Who is the audience for the findings; who will be interested?
- What contribution will your research make to knowledge?
- What is in it for the participants?

## Ethical considerations

The next and most important stage is to consider the ethical implications of your proposed research. Ethics and morals are often confused, but for this book ethics are the guiding principles of what we ought to do, whereas morals are usually concerned with whether something we want to do fits within our society's notion of right and wrong. For example, we may question if it is morally right to use animals instead of humans to test baby food. On the other hand, it would be unethical to test it on the babies.

**ACTIVITY**

Look at the examples of initial ideas for your research; consider the ethical and moral implications of each. Write them down and discuss them with friends and colleagues. Are you all agreed?

Your academic institution will have ethical guidelines, which you must follow. But, it is worth noting the key principles:

- Consent has to be obtained from all who participate in your research; you are not allowed to involve them without their knowledge. If you are involving minors – that is below the age of 16 – permission has to be obtained from their principal carer.
- Consent usually has to be obtained from the most relevant senior person also.
- Nobody should be forced or bribed to take part in research.
- Participants must be made aware of the purpose of your research, and their role in it should be made clear.
- Nobody should be asked to do something that makes them look foolish.
- Your research should not seek to change your participants; that is, they must remain in control of the situation.
- Nobody should be exposed to physical or mental stress.
- Research should never invade someone's privacy.
- Participants should always be treated fairly, equally, and with consideration and respect.
- Everything possible should be done to ensure confidentiality. Again, there are very strict guidelines when working with vulnerable groups such as small children, disabled people and the elderly. This is an issue that should be discussed when seeking permission because there are times when confidentiality may not be appropriate.

- There should be secure methods for processing and storing the data, which should not be kept longer than necessary.

Ethical considerations are complex; you will not be expected as a beginning researcher to be working alone or to have all the answers. It is assumed that your tutor will guide you, but that does not excuse you from acting responsibly and thinking very carefully about the implications of your proposed research.

## Implementation

### Reviewing the literature

Once your initial idea has been approved you move into the implementation process. The first stage of this is to find out what already exists about aspects of this research, and is called reviewing the literature. The searching and storage techniques you learned in Chapter 3 will be very useful here.

Finding out as much as you can about your topic is invaluable. It may give you ideas about methods of gathering data you had not thought about, and it shows you what others have found out or are saying about your topic. Peter tells us, 'I wrote my own summaries and used my notebook, laptop and memory stick. If I liked something I read, I immediately put it on my stick.' Additionally, it makes no sense to invest a lot of time and effort in doing a piece of research only to find out that it has already been done before and your time has been wasted.

There will be times when, no matter how thorough your searching, there appears to be nothing written on the topic. Think creatively; there may be nothing written directly – that is quite likely – but parts of what you are looking at may exist. Use your keywords to find things that might be related to your topic. Remember to make notes about the usefulness of what you have found, which will make sense to you at a later date. Always keep thorough bibliographic references and note down quotations that you may be able to use when writing up your work.

So how do you decide when you have done enough reading and searching? It is impossible to read everything, and if you try to you will never get around to the research itself. You need to keep an eye on your schedule, so take a summary of what you have found and discuss this with your tutor, who will be able to offer you guidance on what is acceptable.

### Choosing the research strategy

Before you can decide which methods to use, you need to be absolutely certain about what you need to know and why, and the amount of time or funding that is available. There may be other constraints you can think of.

Broadly speaking, what you are trying to find out will be:

- Exploratory: you want to find out what is happening and you want to under-stand more. Qualitative methods are usually best for this type of enquiry.
- Descriptive: you want to give an accurate picture of an event, of people, of a situation. You will need a lot of information about the topic that you are going to describe, and either qualitative or quantitative methods could be chosen.
- Explanatory: you want to find an explanation for a situation or a problem and, again, you could use either qualitative or quantitative methods.

Your choice of data collection methods will depend on the way you have designed your research question. The following description of strategies should help you to make your decision.

### Action research

Action research is, essentially, practical problem-solving. It is carried out by a practitioner who has identified a problem in the place of work and seeks to review, evaluate and improve practice. It is carried out over a period of time and may use questionnaires, diaries, observations and so on to collect evidence. This is used to judge the effectiveness of the changes that have been implemented and to make further modifications.

### Case study

Case study is an umbrella term for a whole family of research methods:

- interviews with people;
- checklists of skills, behaviours, abilities, movement, procedures, interactions, resources;
- portfolios of a range of work around a particular topic; a representation of a total experience; a collection of documents for analysis;
- individual files, for example tapes, samples of work, artwork, memos, photos of models or projects and reports;
- diaries or journals written by participants;
- field notes or observation records, or informal notes;
- logs of meetings, lessons, excursions and materials used;
- discussion or interaction – records of comments and thoughts generated by participants;
- questionnaires of attitudes, opinions, preferences, information;
- audio tapes of meetings, discussions about data gathered, games, group work, interviews, groups, monologues, readings, lectures and demonstrations;

- video tapes of participants engaged in their activities;
- still photography of groups working, locations, faces, particular participants over time, at fixed intervals;
- time-on-task analysis of participants; over a lesson, a day, a week.

Two or three methods may be used together to provide an in-depth view of a situation. In this way they cross-check what they are finding. This is called triangulation. Case studies are a good method for individual researchers as they give an opportunity for a thorough study over a limited period of time. Although findings from this type of research cannot be generalised, that is, it cannot be seen as true for all similar situations, case studies are often used successfully to probe issues identified by large surveys.

## Ethnographic research

Anthropologists who wished to study a society or aspects of a society in depth developed the ethnographic style of research. It usually requires the researcher to become partially or totally immersed in the group that is being studied, and to use scrupulous observation. To be successful, the researcher has to become accepted as part of the group, may be doing the same job or living in the same location over a period of time. As a method this has been criticised, partly because of the time it takes but also because it is difficult to say that what the researcher finds is typical of other groups. For example, are Year 3 physics students typical of all Year 3 physics students in the country?

## Surveys

Surveys aim to obtain information that can be analysed to notice trends, make comparisons and find facts. The national census is a survey where the aim is to obtain 100 per cent response. Most surveys are not so ambitious, but this can cause problems because the sample population has to be representative. If, for instance, you wanted to find out if foundation degree students managed their workload, you could not ask all students, but you could take a percentage of each age group, gender and subject studied from various parts of the country.

In surveys, all respondents are asked the same questions and, as far as possible, in the same circumstances. Again, this is not as easy as it seems, questionnaires have to be piloted or tested first to make sure they are clear and unambiguous. Surveys can provide answers to the questions 'What?' 'Where?' When?' and 'How?', but not 'Why?'.

The advantage of surveys is that they can be a relatively cheap and easy way of obtaining large amounts of data. Sometimes, in the case of postal surveys, they are the only way of obtaining information and, of course, because they are anonymous, they encourage more honest answers. The disadvantage is that the response rate on postal and self-administered surveys is very low, and there is no guarantee that the sample represents the population. Other surveys may be influenced by the characteristics and attitudes of the interviewer.

Telephone surveys are becoming increasingly common. They have a high response rate and it is possible to ensure understanding even though there are not the visual clues of a face-to-face interview. Their primary advantages are that distance is no problem; they are low-cost; and they offer safety for both interviewer and interviewee. However, unless you already have a background in statistical analysis, it would be very unwise to undertake a survey as a beginning researcher.

## Experimental methodology

It is reasonably easy to plan an experiment to test something measurable and, of course, most of us are familiar with the concept of laboratory experiments where there are carefully designed procedures. It is also possible to conduct experimental research out of the laboratory, particularly in situations where there is a planned intervention or innovation, such as the introduction of an incentive system for office workers. Studies are based, for example, by comparing data obtained before an intervention and noting the changes that occur as result. Experimental research can also be conducted by exposing one group to a planned intervention and comparing it to a parallel or control group where there has been no intervention, and noting the differences. In this instance there would have to be ethical considerations as one group could be seen as being treated better than the other. Experimental research has to be very carefully planned, but it does allow for conclusions to be drawn about cause and effect. To be regarded as useful research, large groups are needed and, as such, this methodology can be expensive.

## On-line research methods

It is unlikely that you would be expected to undertake on-line research on your own at this stage of your educational career. However, it is worth considering some of the issues surrounding this method of data collection as, clearly, it is a widely used commercial tool.

On-line research usually takes the form of questionnaires to an e-mail address, or interviews that are conducted via e-mail or through internet chat-rooms. Both methods have advantages and disadvantages, which are the same as non-electronic methods. The following are those that are specific to this method only.

### *On-line interviews and questionnaires*
Advantages:

- sent directly, ensuring delivery to recipient;

- easy for respondent to reply, therefore much quicker response;
- few technical skills required;
- novelty encourages larger response.

Disadvantages:

- question design is often simplistic to ensure meaning is clear;
- limited opportunity for interesting graphics;
- valid e-mail addresses are needed, therefore anonymity cannot be assured;
- respondent has to enter data into the database and limited levels of competence may lead to entry error.

According to Eysenbach and Till (2001), definitive ethical guidelines for conducting on-line interviews and questionnaires have not yet been produced for the UK. Therefore you should discuss and agree procedures for the following issues with your tutor:

- Could your research be seen as intrusive?
- Is it possible to create a closed group that requires registration to join to ensure a level of privacy?
- Is the research community you want to contact vulnerable? For example, the mailing list of victims of violent crime or those on drug rehabilitation programmes could be misused if it fell into the wrong hands.
- How can the anonymity of the respondent be protected? You have their e-mail address, so it is possible to find out about them.
- Have intellectual property rights been observed? After all, some respondents might seek publicity.
- Has informed consent been obtained?
- Will the research be valid? The potential for people to be involved in a study may be limited by their access to and knowledge of the internet. This is of particular significance for those wanting to use these methods for international research or with disadvantaged groups.

## Negotiating access

As soon as you have agreed the topic of your research with your tutor, it makes sense to obtain the permission you need to gain access to the organisation, the people and the materials that you need. No matter how well acquainted you may be with the source, it is unwise to expect to be allowed to have access. People are going to be doing you a favour; not only do they need to be fully informed about what it is you are going to do and why, but they also need to have some idea of what they will gain by allowing you to gather data. Be realistic about what you hope to achieve. You might give false hopes, particularly if you are working with people who do not understand research.

Below are some useful tips to help you gain access.

- Request permission formally from the most senior appropriate person. A letter briefly outlining your plans and explaining that the research is part of your degree is often the best approach. Some institutions will ask for your request to be authenticated by your tutor or even a senior member of your academic institution.
- Speak to the people that you want to work with; they also need to know what you are doing and how it will involve them.
- Send an outline plan of the research to the person who gave the initial permission, identifying who will be involved and what they will be doing.
- Remember all the ethical considerations. Talk to your tutor if you are concerned.
- Negotiate and agree what you mean by confidentiality and anonymity. Remember, it may be possible to identify someone, even if you do not use their name.
- Agree who is going to see a copy of the final report and if you are expected to share your findings.
- Be honest with the participants. For example, if you say an interview will only take ten minutes, keep to it.
- As a foundation degree student you are most likely to be conducting your research in your own workplace, so take particular care; you could easily damage your reputation if things do not go as well as expected.
- Dress and behave appropriately for the setting.
- Use your common sense and remember that good manners cost little and open a lot of doors.

## Collecting the data

### Ensuring validity and reliability

There is no point in spending a lot of time planning and carrying out a research project if the data you obtain does not provide you with answers that are valid and reliable. So what do we mean by these terms? To be valid, we need to ask, 'Does the method we are using measure or describe what it is supposed to?'

Decide if the following are valid research methods:

- Using a carefully recorded observation of how many people used a certain chemist shop on a Saturday afternoon in order to ascertain how many people used it per week.

- Interviewing a teacher about a new method of teaching reading to tell you if it is successful.

- Asking members of a Christian group their opinion of extending Sunday opening hours for their local supermarket.

You are quite correct; they are not valid research methods. Make sure you know why.

It is, on the whole, easier to check if your research is reliable; reliability is described as the extent to which the method used produces the same or similar results under identical conditions. For example, questions that ask for opinions can give results that vary from one day to the next.

## Choosing your research sample

In the section on surveys we considered the need to restrict the number of people surveyed. With all investigations the number of subjects we use will depend on the time and resources we have. However, if our data is to be useful we need to think carefully about how we select our sample. Of course, because we depend on goodwill, we may not have total freedom to ensure our sample is perfect, and we will have to rely on what can be called random or opportunity sampling; that is, we use those who are willing and available to us. However, it is important that we mention this in the final report and try to consider how much this may have influenced the data we obtained.

Representative sampling is when the group represents the larger population according to the criteria that will help you find the information you want. If gender and age are important to your investigation of engineering students in your college, you would ensure that you had the correct proportion to the whole in your sample. If you wanted to check the ability of children to read an instruction you would ensure you had equal numbers of boys and girls representing the full span of reading ability within a specific age group. Whether they were tall or short would not be significant, unless you were considering the correct height for school chairs.

Think carefully about your research topic. Talk to colleagues on your course and ask what are the characteristics that are essential to your sample? Are they important?

There are times when you most definitely do not want a representative or random sample. For example, you may wish to interview the only male infant school teacher to gain very specific insights. So be aware that there are many other ways in which a sample can be selected. You might like to investigate this further in Robson (1998).

## Common data collection techniques

It is most likely that you will use some of the methods identified in the section on case studies for your first investigation. In this section we will look more closely at the more common methods with a view to avoiding some of the common traps and pitfalls researchers fall into. If the method you were thinking of using is not mentioned look at the suggestions for further reading and talk to your tutor.

### Observation

Observations can be a very valuable method for data gathering. They can be structured or unstructured, concentrate on action, interaction or dialogue, or a combination, and can be recorded as written notes, ticks on a previously designed recording sheet or electronically. For beginning researchers a structured observation schedule is very helpful. However, there is the danger of the researcher imposing their own ideas about what they should be looking for rather than letting the events speak for themselves.

When making observations you will need to decide which role is most appropriate for you. You can either be a complete observer, sitting or standing somewhere where you have no involvement at all with what you are observing. If you are familiar with the situation, you might be a participant observer, watching at times and at others interacting. For example, you might be watching a physiotherapist working with a group of elderly people. If you know nothing of the techniques involved you would watch; if, however, that is what you are training to do, and the instructor is happy for you to join in, you might help some of the participants. If you want to observe as a complete participant you would most likely join the class.

### Interviews

#### *Single-person interview*

Advantages:

- detailed information and opinions can be gathered;
- can be conducted in a mutually convenient and non-threatening setting;
- questions can be re-phrased or explained if not understood;

- the interviewer can note ways in which the response is made, such as tone of voice and facial expression;
- good when respondents cannot read or write adequately for the level of questioning.

Disadvantages:

- respondent may try to please the interviewer;
- some interview settings can be very distracting;
- ethical issues of one-to-one interviews must be addressed;
- the interviewer may show a bias towards a certain viewpoint through their body language;
- recording interviews by hand can be distracting for the interviewer. Electronic recording is costly and time-consuming to transcribe;
- wording of questions is critical.

### *Group interviews*

Advantages:

- enable more data to be collected at once;
- may stimulate others' views;
- group members may feel less threatened.

Disadvantages

- some members might influence others;
- need careful control; discussions can go off the point;
- recording can be difficult.

The advantages and disadvantages of telephone interviews are the same as they are for telephone surveys. Additionally, recording can be difficult.

Interviews fall broadly into three categories. In structured interviews there is a schedule of questions like a questionnaire, to which the interviewer records the answers. This is a good technique for beginner researchers as it ensures they ask the same thing each time. It is also helpful for interviewing people who might find it difficult to read a questionnaire.

A semi-structured interview has a schedule of questions, but the interviewee has an opportunity to respond to each in their own way. Analysing the data from this type of interview is more difficult, but the data is more exciting.

In unstructured interviews only the topic is chosen. This is an excellent technique in skilled hands as the data can be really valuable, but it takes expertise to control and is very difficult to analyse.

When you are designing your interview schedule, as a general rule you should start with the simple easy-to-answer questions to put your respondents at their ease, then progress to the more difficult ones and finish with ones where respondents' opinions are important because, by then, they should be more relaxed. Run a pilot before doing the proper research. This will give you an idea of whether it works and ensure it does not become too long.

Your job as an interviewer is to get people to talk freely and openly. To do this you should listen more than you speak; put questions in a clear, straightforward and non-threatening manner; avoid giving clues about your viewpoint; and enjoy the experience. Try to vary your voice and facial expression and try to avoid looking bored.

During your preparation for this part of your degree, you should have some interviewer assessment and training where your tutor or colleagues can provide valuable feedback. Additionally, a recording or video can enable self-evaluation.

### *Questionnaires*

Advantages:

- questions require very careful wording;
- not too time-consuming;
- anonymity of respondent is assured;
- data collector remains detached;
- can reach a large number of people;
- easy to analyse.

Disadvantages:

- no opportunities for clarification of questions;
- reproduction cost;
- cannot probe interesting responses;
- recipient must be able to read and write proficiently;
- poor response rate.

There are many ways in which a questionnaire can be designed. The design will depend on what you want to find out. Responses can be:

- nominal: identifying your answer from a pre-determined list;
- ordinal or Likert: for example, 'Foundation degree students should study statistics'. Strongly agree/Agree/Not certain/Disagree/Strongly disagree;
- interval scales: 'What is your age?' Below 21/21–26/27–35/36–45/46–54/ over 55. Circle one;
- ranked responses: for example, 'Rate the following museums and galleries visited in order of preference'. Give 1 for the best and 4 for the least useful.
  Tate Modern
  National Gallery

Victoria and Albert Museum

Tate Britain;

- Semantic differential: for example, place a tick on the line to show your opinion of the college accommodation:

clean_____ dirty.

Think about interviews you have taken part in or questionnaires you have completed and how frustrated you have felt when you were not able to squeeze your answer into the box, or the questions were not the ones you would have asked. It is really important that you think about the way you design the questionnaire. The most common faults are:

- leading the question; asking it in a way that tells the respondent the answer;
- double questions; these give two or more choices, which may conflict;
- some questions use words that are not very precise;
- some questions are so complex they are impossible to answer properly;
- hearsay questions ask about things of which the respondent is unlikely to have evidence, only opinion; and
- closed questions, which lead only to yes or no answers.

---

**ACTIVITY**

Consider the following questions from a questionnaire. Which common traps and pitfalls can you identify? Can you think of another way of phrasing them?

- How much time do you spend on travelling? A great deal/quite a lot/not much.
- Which type of school does your child go to? Infant/Primary/Secondary/Comprehensive/Grammar/Other.
- Do you think your colleagues like to learn?
- Do you like to travel by train or bus?
- Should examinations at the end of compulsory schooling be easier or more difficult now?
- Do you agree that men are more suited to a career in engineering?
- What do you think of the new government policy on early years education?

---

## Drawing conclusions from the data

The raw data you have obtained from your interviews, observations and so on may be fascinating, but it is not a lot of use if it is not in a presentable form. This is where the painstaking work begins. You are looking for similarities and differences, groupings, patterns and so on. You have had ideas based on your experience about the responses before you collected the data, and you will have been careful to eliminate your bias.

If you are involved in a larger research project, which has used surveys for data collection, or you have experience with statistics, you may like to use computer software such as the Statistical Package for Social Science (SPSS). Your academic institution's learning resources centre will be able to advise you of training opportunities and may well provide you with the most up-to-date version.

## Coding and presenting data

Coding is the process of organising the data into an analysable form. This applies to both quantitative and qualitative methods. Finding the best method to code your data is largely a matter of common sense, and as you become experienced it makes sense to think about it when you are designing the research method.

As a rule, quantitative data is coded by letters or numbers which can then be analysed without referring to the question (see Figure 5.1); or it can be translated by hand into a tally sheet (see Figure 5.2). This will give you a picture of the age of your respondents, which could then be turned into a bar chart, pie chart or a simple table. These are easy to manage, with or without a computer, and can help to make interpretation simpler. Stephen (2006) is very helpful and an excellent source for tables, charts etc.

| Age identification could be coded on the questionnaire and then entered into a computer-based spreadsheet | | | | | | |
|---|---|---|---|---|---|---|
| 21–25 | 26–30 | 31–35 | 35–40 | 41–45 | 46–50 | over 50 |
| 1 | 2 | 3 | 4 | 5 | 6 | 7 please circle one |

**FIGURE 5.1** Coding quantitative data on a questionnaire

| 21–25 | 26–30 | 31–35 | 35–40 | 41–45 | 46–50 | over 50 |
|---|---|---|---|---|---|---|
| 1111 | 1111 | 1111 | 1111 | 1111 | 1111 | 11 |
| | 1111 | 1111 | 1111 | 11 | 1 | |
| | 1111 | 1111 | 1111 | | | |
| | | 1111 | 111 | | | |
| | | 11 | | | | |
| 5 | 15 | 22 | 18 | 7 | 6 | 2 |

**FIGURE 5.2** A tally sheet

Interpreting qualitative data follows a similar procedure but you have to read the data first to create the categories. For example, a research student asked pupils what they thought about abstract paintings before she taught a series of lessons in an art gallery (see Table 5.1). She took their initial responses, turned them into categories and then asked them to rate the categories at the end of the project to identify the impact of her teaching.

**TABLE 5.1** Pupils' thoughts and feelings about abstract paintings

|  | Prior to the project | | After the project | |
|  | yes | no | yes | no |
| --- | --- | --- | --- | --- |
| I do not understand anything | 12 | 12 | 5 | 19 |
| I move on to the next work | 17 | 7 | 9 | 15 |
| I am annoyed | 9 | 15 | 4 | 20 |
| I am not interested in it | 10 | 14 | 5 | 19 |
| I want to laugh | 12 | 12 | 5 | 19 |
| I try to understand what it represents | 7 | 17 | 21 | 3 |
| I like it | 12 | 12 | 22 | 2 |

Interpreting data from semi-structured questions is much the same, but numbers of responses are not recorded. You might look for units of meaning, for example interviewees were asked about the benefits of including craft in the school curriculum. What they said could be coded into the following broad categories:

- Intrinsic benefits: hands on, uses different intelligence, tangible outcome, independent learning.
- Extrinsic benefits: develops higher-order thinking skills, interactive and collaborative learning, transfer of learning, vocational outcome.

You could look for particular words, phrases or topics that have relevance to your research.

## Analysing data

**ACTIVITY**

Look at Table 5.1, 'Pupils' thoughts and feelings about abstract paintings'. What conclusions could you draw?

Overall, you can see that the intervention has had some level of success in that the pupils appear more willing to try to understand the paintings. However, we would have to view this data with a degree of caution because it is possible that the pupils were particularly willing to try the exercise since they knew that they were part of a research project. This phenomenon is known as the 'Hawthorne Effect'.

Analysing the data is the central part of the research. Fortunately, there is a wide range of approaches and techniques available. Deciding which to use is not easy but sensible decisions pay dividends in the end. As a beginner, it makes sense therefore to keep in close contact with your research tutor and to take note of their suggestions. Like everything else in your degree, research can seem daunting at the beginning, but it is exciting and you will improve with practice. In the following chapter you will find some useful tips on writing your final report.

## ■ Websites to visit for more information

www.admin.ex.ac.uk/academic/ethics2/ – for discussion of ethical issues.
www.bath.ac.uk/e-learning/gold/glossary.html#indexOf – entries for glossary of research methods terms.
www.federalsurrey.ac.uk/researcherscompanion/fif/134ab.asp – excellent site for beginning tutorial on research.
www.nottingham.ac.uk/education/information-for-students/research-ethics/reading-list.phtml/ – good for information on ethics of research.
www.soc.surrey.ac.uk/sru – *Social Research Up-Date*, issue 11 on visual research methods.

## ■ Recommended reading

Birley, G. and Moreland, N. (1998) *A Practical Guide to Academic Research*. London: Kogan Page.
Denzin, N. and Lincoln, Y. (eds) (2000) *Handbook of Qualitative Research* (2nd edn). London: Sage.
Foddy, W. (1995) *Constructing Questions for Interviews and Questionnaires*. Cambridge: Cambridge University Press.
Trochim, W. (2005) *Ethics in Research*. London: Sage.

## ■ References

Bell, J. (1995) *Doing Your Research Project: A Guide for First Time Researchers in Education and Social Science* (2nd edn). Buckingham: Open University Press.
Eysenbach, G. and Till, J.E. (2001) 'Ethical issues in qualitative research on internet communities'. *British Medical Journal*, **323** (7321), 1103–5.
Robson, C. (1998) *Real World Research: A Resource for Social Scientists and Practitioners*. London: Blackwell.
Stephen, M. (2006) *Teach Yourself Basic Computer Skills*. London: McGraw-Hill.

# 6 Effective academic writing techniques: producing your first essay

Success on most foundation degree courses will depend, to a large extent, on the quality of the written material you submit. While presentations and other forms of assessment will, of course, play a part, if you look at your course handbook you will see that you are expected to produce written work in the form of assignments. Some may be professionally oriented, such as business and laboratory reports, accounts of field trips and book reviews; this mode of writing is designed to address the needs of your specific vocational situation. Other writing will be more academic, such as essays and dissertations, which aim to focus on debates about theoretical perspectives.

Although each of these types of writing has specific conventions, what they have in common is that they require you to develop a writing style that may be very different from that which you are used to. For your degree you will be expected to answer specific questions and to present your evidence in a logical sequence. You will need to deal with conflicting arguments and take a precise and objective stance – quite a challenge for even the most confident and experienced writer.

Everyone struggles with writing their first essay, so we will start here by taking you through the process, step by step. We will also consider what a good writing style actually looks like, giving tips on what you should include and some pitfalls to avoid. Finally, we take a brief look at some forms of writing, such as reports and dissertations, and give suggestions for further reading. You will not be able to achieve an effortless academic writing style straight away; your tutors' comments on your written work will help you to develop your writing over the course of your foundation degree. Indeed, when you look back over your studies you may find that your ability to write more effectively is one of your most significant achievements.

## Writing your first essay

### Managing the essay writing process

Although styles of essays do vary to some extent between subject areas, there are some basic techniques that apply. This section takes you through the step-by-step process of writing your first essay, from starting with a title to getting the essay back from your tutor. Writing an essay is not one task; it is several, and you need to plan the process so that you allow adequate time for each step. As soon as you get your first essay title, you need to start thinking about what is required, so that you can focus your reading and begin to make notes about anything that might be useful. Maria recommends that you 'allow plenty of time to gather information and ask for help from your mentor'.

An early start is essential. Often the assessments from different modules have the same deadlines and you will have to learn to juggle your tasks, so the sooner you start the better. It avoids stress in the longer term and helps you present the best possible piece of work you can accomplish at this stage of your degree. You really should allow several days to write your first essay, so plan your time carefully. Sara recommends that you 'start early and have tutorials with your tutor. Get clear advice on referencing.' Pauline suggests that you 'use your time wisely, gather information and start work promptly. Don't leave it to the last minute or you will have sleepless nights.'

Before you start you should read your programme handbook carefully, and check the following points with your tutor if you have any queries:

- What is the word length? How flexible is this?
- Is it acceptable to use sub-headings in the essay to divide up certain points? Views on this vary from discipline to discipline.
- What is the view on the use of 'I' – the first person – in essays?
- What format of referencing is required? Should a bibliography also be included?
- What are the criteria for assessment? These should be written down in your handbook. Check that you have a copy.

## Analyse the question

The essay title will set you thinking about the material you have been studying. It is essential to show by your final paragraph that you have answered the question, or completed the task posed by the title. Jeremy suggests you need to 'be sure to read the questions carefully. Write important and valuable things to cover the necessary criteria.' It is important, when you first receive your essay title, to pick out the key words. Remember how you learned to do this in Chapter 3. These fall into two categories:

- content-related words, which give you an idea of what you should write about, setting useful parameters; and
- procedure-related words, which tell you what approach you should use.

Example essay title: 'Describe the principal methods of controlling substances hazardous to health at work. Evaluate how effective these are in an organisation with which you are familiar'. The key content words in this example are: 'controlling substances', 'hazardous to health', 'organisation', and 'familiar'. The key procedure words are: 'describe' and 'evaluate'.

**ACTIVITY**

Write down the essay title you have been given and circle the key content-related words. Now look for the procedure-related words from the list below. Do you understand exactly what you have been asked to do by your tutor? Check any words in the title you do not understand in a dictionary, encyclopaedia or a general reference text for your subject, and write down their definitions.

*Key procedure-related words*

- account for: give a good explanation of something and evaluate possible causes / reasons;
- analyse: examine the topic by dividing it into parts, look at each part in detail, form judgements about each element and the whole;
- argue: provide reasons for and / or against something, in an appropriate order, citing evidence, which may be other people's research, or other kinds of facts and information;
- assess: judge the significance of something, referring to the special knowledge of experts wherever possible, that is, referring to or quoting from other people's work;
- comment on: give your own opinion about something, supported by reasons and evidence;
- compare: examine one thing in relation to something else, to emphasise points of difference or similarity;
- contrast: explore the differences between the items or arguments mentioned;
- criticise: discuss the good and / or bad qualities of theories or opinions, supporting your judgement with reasons and evidence;
- define: explain the exact meaning of a word or phrase;
- describe: give a detailed account of different aspects, points of view, parts, characteristics or qualities;
- discuss: consider something by writing about it from different points of view with supporting evidence;
- distinguish: look for differences between;
- enumerate: list and mention items separately in number order;

- evaluate: calculate the value, validity or effectiveness of a theory, decision or object, including your own opinion, and supporting each point with evidence of specific facts, details or reasons;
- examine: critically explore the opinion or argument;
- explain: give reasons how and why to account for something, so that it is clear and easy to understand;
- illustrate: use examples or diagrams to make explicit;
- interpret: give your own opinion of the significance of something, citing reasons and evidence wherever possible;
- justify: give good reasons for decisions or conclusions, perhaps by referring to other texts;
- narrate: indicate what has happened, as if telling a story;
- outline: give the main features of or, facts or general idea about something, omitting minor details;
- prove: show something is accurate, true or valid by using facts, documents and/or other information to build your case;
- reconcile: show how apparently conflicting things can appear similar or compatible;
- relate: establish how things are connected or associated, how they affect each other or how they are alike;
- review: examine an area and assess it critically;
- show: explain something giving evidence or examples to establish a strong case;
- state: put something clearly and concisely; support each point with specific facts or details;
- summarise: give a brief, concise account of the main points of something leaving out details and examples;
- to what extent: consider how far something is true or not true;
- trace: follow the cause or stages in development of something in chronological order from its start.

## Gathering your ideas together

There will be time for reading what others have to say about the topic later. Now is the time for some thinking. When gathering your ideas you should note down everything you think about the topic, without stopping to consider the merit of each idea. It is creative, easy, and you will begin to get some ideas down on paper. Kerry suggests that you 'do little spidergrams of areas you want to write about in your assignments'. It is essential that you now begin writing your ideas down, even if you later scrap most of what you write at this early stage. As your list gets longer you will begin to feel more confident about writing your essay.

---

**ACTIVITY**

Take your annotated essay title and write it in the middle of a large sheet of paper. Now jot down any thoughts at all as they come to you. A good way to do this is on large post-it notes, as you can later move these around into some form of structure. Write quickly and uncritically. If you prefer, you can use a mind map to complete this task. For further information on mind mapping see Chapter 3. If you are stuck for ideas try and jot down thoughts about:

- points for and against the question in the title;
- what each of the key content and procedure words means;
- which areas you need to develop;
- what examples of illustrations you can give;
- what reading you need to do; and
- which areas need references.

---

## Producing an essay plan

Now that you have plenty of ideas, it is important to get them into some kind of shape. At this early stage in your studies this does not have to be over-complex; you could start by simply listing points for and against any particular question. It is important that you always try to bring the following elements into your work:

- State your topic, idea or hypothesis, this is called the 'topic sentence'.
- Support your ideas by using evidence.
- Explain how the evidence supports what you say, and carry out some analysis; for example, you could look at how far the evidence supports or opposes the topic sentence.

Each part of the essay structure will be considered in more detail later in this chapter, but you should be mindful of Aristotle's advice on writing classical drama that there should be a beginning, a middle and an end. Essays should always present a logical sequence of ideas, and you should use information as evidence to support or contradict your point of view. A sound essay shows that you can see more than one side to a question. This is a good way to demonstrate your ability to analyse and evaluate information. Demonstrating these skills is usually necessary to get high marks. You should show that your argument is based on evidence, not unsubstantiated opinion. The argument should flow through the title, from sentence to sentence, to the conclusion, without any breaks. We offer some hints on how to structure your essay into key paragraphs in the next section (p.87).

A structure might be:

- introduction, to tell the reader what you are going to do;
- first argument for – state, support, explain;
- second argument for – state, support, explain;
- first argument against – state, support, explain;
- second argument against – state support, explain;
- make judgements on evidence;
- conclusions;
- references and bibliography. This is covered in detail in Chapter 7.

Alternatively, your structure could be:

- introduction (200 words);
- state main topic 1: evidence for/against, explain (400 words);
- state main topic 2: evidence for/against, explain (400 words);
- state main topic 3: evidence for/against, explain (400 words);
- make judgements on evidence (300 words);
- conclusions (300 words);
- references and bibliography.

At this stage you may also want to allocate a rough word count against each section, as in the example above for a 2,000-word essay. This is arbitrary, but it may help you keep within the word count. Your academic institution will usually tolerate a 10 per cent variation on the word count, but may penalise you if you stray more than this. Now have a go with your ideas from the idea-gathering exercise.

**ACTIVITY**

Take the post-it notes with your ideas on; try and organise them into sets of arguments, evidence or comment. These will eventually be your paragraphs. Can you see a logical sequence gradually emerging? Now summarise this into your essay plan.

## Targeted reading

You now need to do some reading, and the best place to start is with the notes you have made and the handouts you have been given. At this stage in your foundation degree your tutor is likely to be concerned about whether you understand the course content. Look at the suggestions for further reading but don't spend too long reading; make sure you allow sufficient time for writing the essay.

---

**ACTIVITY**

Now is the time to read purposefully. Do not be side-tracked – search systematically for evidence to support your arguments.

Make very brief notes of what you have found in the appropriate place in your essay plan and note down references.

Revise the order of your essay plan if necessary.

---

## Writing your first draft

The last activity asked you to revise the structure of your essay plan in the light of your reading. It is acceptable to change your mind about what you are writing; it proves that you are learning something from your reading. Similarly, what you write in your first draft will invariably get changed. The key is to make a start and write something down; this will reduce the stress you are probably feeling, give you something to refine and tell you what more you need to find out. It is important not to try for perfection at the first attempt, just write. Charles advises that, 'the worst part is putting pen to paper. Once you get started it's not as bad as you think it is. Always ask for help if you're struggling.'

### Writing your opening paragraph

This seems the obvious place to start, but we suggest that you leave the detail of this until you have finished drafting the rest of the essay. Your introductory and concluding paragraphs are the most important, so we suggest you read through this section, start work on the main body, then come back and write the introduction at the end.

The most important point we would make is that under no circumstances should you merely repeat the essay title. Paraphrasing the question is empty and unnecessary. Instead, make sure you:

- say what the essay will do – look back at the procedure-related words here and list the key stages of the essay so that the reader knows what to expect and in which order;

- establish some control over the subject – perhaps you wish to focus on a specific area or contest a particular viewpoint;
- indicate why the topic of the essay is important or interesting, perhaps making reference to some published work or a range of arguments about the subject.

These are the basic principles, and you can use them in any order. You could also consider beginning with:

- a quotation – this can address the third point above and, if chosen well, can be an interesting and lively way to start; or
- a definition – again this is acceptable, but make sure you say something about the definition and so take control; perhaps, for example, there are several different definitions. This then would be worthy of comment. Use this technique with care.

### Writing the main body of your essay

Here you need to follow the plan you made, writing paragraph by paragraph to ensure that you bring out the key points. Remember that you are looking to state, support and explain; so always check that every point you make is supported by evidence. This evidence must be accurately referenced (see Chapter 7 for further details).

Does your argument hold together? Your essay must move convincingly from point to point. In most essays, sub-headings are not used, although they some-times are in the social sciences or for very long essays, so check with your tutor. This means that you need to write your paragraphs carefully so that they are self-contained, that is, they are about one topic or element in the argument. Then give them coherence by linking them together to develop the argument in a way that is clear for the reader to follow. One way to do this is to begin a new paragraph with a link back to the previous one, then connect that in some way with the new topic.

Links can be of many different kinds, you might want to:

- add something on to what you've just said, using words such as 'again', 'also', 'as well as', 'and', 'furthermore', 'in addition', 'moreover' and 'next';
- show some form of contrast to what you've said: 'although', 'but', 'despite', 'even though', 'however', 'on the contrary', 'on the other hand', 'neverthe-less', 'yet';
- make a concession: 'although', 'even though', 'however', 'whilst';
- give examples: 'as an illustration', 'for example', 'for instance', 'in this case', 'namely', 'one example is';
- emphasise: 'certainly', 'definitely', 'especially', 'indeed', 'in fact', 'particu-larly', 'unquestionably', 'without doubt';

- show argument: 'although', 'as a result', 'at this point', 'because', 'consequently', 'evidently', 'hence', 'however', 'moreover', 'since', 'therefore', 'thus';

- conclude: 'as a conclusion', 'as has been stated', 'finally', 'in general', 'in short', 'on the whole', 'to sum up'.

**ACTIVITY**

Now write the main body of your essay, following your essay plan. Just do the best you can; there should be time left for redrafting later. If you get stuck with your writing have a look at the section on how to deal with writer's block below.

## Writing a concluding paragraph

Your first and last impressions are crucial; you need to show your reader that you have answered the question, and the easiest way to do this is to return directly to the essay title, using one of the conclusion links above. You must make your viewpoint clear here by briefly restating your argument, perhaps putting in a last quote, then making a final judgement in your own words. If you do use a quotation, don't let the quote speak for you; you should be in control of the essay. Other interesting endings include:

- a very short final sentence to contrast with your detailed argument earlier in the essay;

- a comment about gaps in current knowledge or putting your argument into a wider context.

**ACTIVITY**

Now write your final paragraph, then go back and write your opening paragraph. Put your writing away, at least overnight. Do not hand your work in; it will almost certainly need redrafting.

## Dealing with writer's block

If you feel anxious about your writing, it is quite possible you will suffer from writer's block, where the words just will not come. Everyone suffers from it at times. Here are some tips about how to beat it:

- Distract yourself by doing something completely different. Positive suggestions include taking a relaxing bath, going outside for a walk or doing some work in the garden. Realistically, most distractions are not that healthy and include watching TV, reading a magazine or, curiously, housework, like ironing or washing up. It does not matter what displacement activity you choose, just stop writing and do something completely different for at least half an hour.

- Reading your work aloud often helps you make amendments to what you have written. By proofreading and amending your existing work you may get back into writing again.

- Write a paragraph, or write for 15 minutes without correcting your words, then allow yourself to stop and do something completely different.

- Try leaving a sentence or paragraph unfinished; that way you can start off your next writing session fairly easily.

- Try explaining the structure of your essay to a friend or a family member. You will probably need to simplify your ideas and language, and their enthusiasm might give you some ideas and motivate you to start writing again.

## Writing your second draft

You now need to revise your first draft. To do so, you must ask yourself the following questions:

- Does the essay have an effective introduction and conclusion? These are key areas to work on as they are the first and last things your reader will see, so go back and tighten up your writing.

- Is your argument always supported by evidence? Do not skimp on this. Is there any final reading you need to do?

- Does your argument flow clearly? You may need to move your paragraphs about here and look at the way you link them.

**ACTIVITY**

Go through the three points listed above and amend your work as necessary. You are now ready to proofread your work.

Before you do the final proofread you should read and check your essay against the next section.

## ■ Writing for academic purposes

You will note that in writing this book we do not always follow our own guidance on writing for academic purposes. This is because we are writing what we hope is an informal and helpful guide rather than an essay or a dissertation.

There are a number of accepted conventions that you should follow when writing for academic purposes. Much comes down to writing in a quite formal but, hopefully, readable and interesting style. The following are things to look out for.

### Personal or impersonal?

One of the most common questions asked by students is whether it is appropriate to write in the 'first person', that is, using 'I'. Academic writing should be based on reason and argument, so generally you should avoid using personal pronouns such as 'I' and 'we' as this can appear subjective and biased. This is called using the passive voice; for example, 'It may be considered...', rather than the active voice, 'I consider...'.

However, the situation here is complicated and there is no straightforward, correct answer. In some subjects, particularly education and the arts, you may be expected to write about your personal experience or apply academic work to your own practice, while disciplines such as science are usually much less personal. Regardless of subject, you will need to write in a balanced, informed way. The best way to tackle this is to check with your tutor first as, in our experience, many tutors have strong views on this question.

### Take care with emphasis

As we have just outlined, academic writing focuses on intellect rather than emotion so you need to take care when you wish to emphasise a point. Do avoid subjective, personal words such as 'great', 'nice', 'unusual', which may mean something very different to your reader than to you. We would also suggest you should not:

- use bigger type to emphasise something;
- use bold or italics to emphasise a point;
- put in exclamations like 'cool'; or
- use exclamation marks.

## Avoid colloquialisms and slang

A colloquialism is any feature of language that is commonly used in speech but not in writing, except perhaps in e-mails and informal notes. Slang words, like the exclamation 'cool!' are not appropriate to use in academic argument.

- Contractions – words like 'they're' for 'they are', or 'isn't' for 'is not', should be avoided and written out in full.
- Abbreviations should be avoided. Again, write words out in full. Use 'for example', not 'e.g.'; 'that is', not 'i.e.', etc. You should avoid 'etc.' and also the ampersand '&' for 'and' – neither belong in formal academic writing.

## Always write in sentences

A sentence is a self-contained unit of meaning, starting with a capital letter and ending with a full stop or question mark. As a minimum it has a verb – a 'doing' word – and a subject, a person or thing that is carrying out the 'doing'. By reading your work aloud you should be able to tell whether your sentences can stand by themselves or whether something is missing. This practical ability to judge what works is more important than a detailed knowledge of the rules of grammar. Another way to check is to use your word-processing package's grammar checking facility – in Microsoft Word you should click on Tools and then Spelling and Grammar.

## Understand how to punctuate

Here is a very brief guide to some of the punctuation issues we think are important and that are sometimes overlooked by students. We have recommended a number of books to help you with punctuation, grammar and style at the end of this chapter. The most accessible, and amusing, is *Eats, Shoots & Leaves* by Lynne Truss (2003).

## Use of capital letters

The rule here is that proper nouns – words that name specific persons, places or things, such as Dorothy Bedford and Liz Wilson, Roehampton University – require capital letters, whereas common nouns – words that identify general categories, such as teachers or university – are not capitalised. Acronyms – such as HE or APEL, where each letter stands for a whole word – should also be capitalised and the full term included in the text.

## Use of apostrophes

The two main uses of apostrophes are to indicate possession, or the omission of letters or numbers. When an 's' is put at the end of the word to indicate possession or ownership, there should always be an apostrophe before it. The exception is if the word already ends in an 's' because it is plural. In this case you add the apostrophe to indicate possession, but not another 's', for example, 'students' union'.

We have explained above that contractions, such as 'wasn't', should not be used in academic writing as they are too informal. However, it is quite acceptable to use an apostrophe in everyday writing to indicate that you have left letters out.

## Other punctuation marks

There are few rules for the use of a comma, as its use is often a matter of taste or emphasis. The basic function of a comma is to separate words, phrases or clauses in a sentence, when a slight pause is required for sense. You might be able to appreciate this better if you read your work aloud. Many writers over-use commas in a way that interrupts the flow of a sentence, you should use a comma only when it contributes something to the sense.

Question-marks are the alternative way to end a sentence. They have the force of a full stop and should be followed by a capital letter. Do not use a question mark and a full stop.

## Spelling

You should always use your word processor's spellchecker before you submit any piece of coursework. However, be aware that a spellchecker does not pick up properly spelled words that may be incorrect in your particular context, 'fro' instead of 'for', for example, or 'there' instead of 'their'. These latter words are known as 'homophones'; they sound alike but have different spellings and meanings.

**ACTIVITY**

Look at the list of homophones below and make sure you can define them. If you are not sure, then look up the answers in a dictionary and make a note for future use:

| | |
|---|---|
| cite/sight/site | practice/practise |
| complement/compliment | principal/principle |
| discreet/discrete | stationary/stationery |

As you cannot rely on a spellchecker, it is essential to make time to read your work through, preferably aloud, before submission. Reading aloud can really help you to spot mistakes, particularly missing words and repetitions. If you have used any word you are not sure of, look it up in a dictionary.

**ACTIVITY**

Ask someone to read you the list of commonly misspelled words below, and check how many you can spell accurately. It is worth keeping a list of the mistakes you make most often in the back of a diary or file and adding to it as necessary.

| | | | |
|---|---|---|---|
| accommodation | advertisement | aesthetic | assessor |
| beginning | calendar | coefficient | commitment |
| comparative | definite | dilemma | grammar |
| government | independence | knowledge | liaise |
| lieutenant | omission | precede | privilege |
| psychology | restaurant | sentence | sergeant |
| sincerely | supersede | separate | unnecessary |

## Avoid discriminatory language

You should not use language that discriminates against people in your academic writing, and this means you need to think consciously about sexism, racism and disability. Much discriminatory language is unintentional, and here are some hints on how to write appropriately in your work:

- Do not use words that assume all people are male: 'people' is better than 'mankind', reception can be 'staffed' rather than 'manned'. Often this means you may have to use the phrase 'he or she', or the plural 'they'.
- Avoid using job titles that assume the person is male or female. Use 'supervisor' rather than 'foreman', for example, or 'police officer' rather than 'policeman'.
- Avoid using racist and disablist language. Again, this is often done in ignorance. Have a look at the British Sociological Association's guidelines on language, which you will find under quality and ethics resources on www.britsoc.co.uk. They also have useful information about non-sexist language.

## ▌ Essential checklist before submission of any written work

This section assumes you have followed the guidance throughout this chapter and have presented the essay in the form of an argument that answers the question in a way that is supported by evidence. Even so, it is essential that you leave time, and make the effort, to proofread your work before handing in. Proofreading can improve your mark significantly, moving your work into the next grade boundary. Do not attempt to proofread on screen; print off a copy of your work.

- Is the essay written in a proper academic style? You should go through all the points mentioned in the last section. Check especially for spelling and punctuation mistakes.
- Is the essay well presented in the format requested by the tutor; for example double-line spacing and wide margins?
- Does every sentence make sense? Remember the best way to proofread is to read your work aloud.
- Have you used your secondary sources properly? We will cover plagiarism in Chapter 7.
- Have you kept to the word limit?
- Are your references and bibliography in a proper format? This has not been covered here but is dealt with in detail in Chapter 7.

**ACTIVITY**

Complete your final proofreading, print off your essay, saving a final copy and hand it in on time. Well done!

## Learning from feedback

Writing your first essay is a major achievement, and we hope you have learned from the advice in this chapter. Your first essay is just that, probably your first attempt at academic writing at HE level 1, and what matters is that you have done your best. There is no expectation that your work will be perfect, whatever that means. If you would like further help with essay writing then you should contact your academic institution's learning support services.

Writing essays and getting feedback from your tutor is the best way of learning your craft. Look at the assessment criteria for your piece of work alongside your tutor's comments. Don't just file your essay away in your folder; spend time thinking about the feedback from your tutor, considering what they have identified as your strengths and also your areas for development. Add these to your proofreading checklist above so that these comments make a difference to your next piece of work.

## ■ Tips for writing reports and other assignments

Much of what has been written above applies to a wide range of other writing you will have to do for your foundation degree. However, as your degree encompasses both vocational and academic learning it is likely, at some stage, that you will have to write a report, both for your study and at work, as reports are a common method of conveying information in the business world.

Structures for reports vary, and you need to seek guidance from your tutor or manager if they have any preferences. However, many reports have the following sections:

- Front sheet with, as a minimum, the report title, author and date.
- Contents page listing all the main headings together with their page numbers.
- Summary or abstract covering the main findings, conclusions and recommendations, usually on one side of A4.
- Introduction to give a clear statement of purpose.
- Background, setting the report in context.
- Methodology outlining how the investigation will take place. What primary and secondary research will be conducted? See Chapter 5 for more guidance on these terms. Headings and sub-headings should be used throughout the report.
- Findings should be presented in a logical sequence, moving from the descriptive to the analytical. Directly relevant figures and tables should be included here, background material should go in the appendices.
- Conclusions should pick up the themes introduced in the introduction and show what has been established. No new information should be included here.
- Recommendations for further action should be identified. These should follow in a logical sequence.
- Appendices should contain any directly relevant background material; for example, a copy of the questionnaire used to collect the data.
- The bibliography should contain books, articles, internet publications and other sources that have been used to compile the report.

## Writing a dissertation

Some foundation degrees require a dissertation or project to be produced, often as a final piece of work, although this is more common at honours degree level. This is a valuable test of your ability to carry out a major piece of research. The academic writing techniques described earlier in this chapter will contribute to your success, but detailed guidance is beyond the scope of this book, although you will find useful techniques for data gathering in Chapter 5. If your foundation degree includes the production of a dissertation we suggest you look at the books in the further reading section for guidance.

## ■ Recommended reading

King, G. (2000) *Punctuation*. Glasgow: HarperCollins.
*A clearly written guide to punctuation, part of the Collins Wordpower series.*
Lashley, C. and Best, W. (2001) *12 Steps to Study Success*. London and New York: Continuum, pp. 175–202.
*A clear introduction to what is required in writing a dissertation.*
Phythian, B. A. (2003) *Teach Yourself Correct English* (revised by Rowe, A.). London: Hodder & Stoughton.
*A useful, accessible book divided into two parts, the first dealing with rules and the second offering advice on using language, including essay, letter and report writing tips.*
Truss, L. (2003) *Eats, Shoots & Leaves: The Zero Tolerance Approach to Punctuation*. London: Profile Books.
*A wonderful, yet educational, rant on the use and misuse of punctuation.*
White, B. (2003) *Dissertation Skills for Business and Management Students*. London: Thomson Learning.

# 7 How to make quotations, citations and a bibliography and avoid plagiarism

In the previous chapter we considered how to improve your academic writing. This chapter looks at ways of enhancing your writing still further, without running the risk of plagiarising or copying other people's work.

All writing is tailored to an audience and obeys certain principles. One of the key differences in academic writing is that it is solely intended to enlarge the understanding of a topic for the reader. Therefore your writing should contain information from other sources as well. This enhances your reader's understanding and enables them to consult the sources if they wish. You may have assumed that the purpose of your learning to write academically is to enable your lecturer to ascertain your level of knowledge and understanding and check your background reading. To an extent this is the case, but it is also to prepare you for the time when you may be making a contribution to the learning of others.

## Acknowledging sources of information

You are expected to refer in your writing to ideas and material from other sources, which may include theories, points of view, diagrams, tables, research, statistics etc. All the sources must be acknowledged and professionally referenced. These are also called 'citations'. Citations must be referenced in the text itself and at the end in the bibliography. You need them when you:

- quote: use exact words from another source;
- summarise: sum up ideas or arguments from another source;
- paraphrase: use the material from another source in your own words; and
- copy: use illustrations, diagrams, maps, tables, charts etc.

This activity is not something to leave to the end of your writing; it is an integral part of your work, and the process of referencing will help you to develop your ideas. Make referencing as you go along one of your golden rules of writing.

The procedures for citing references vary from one academic institution to the next. These will be included in your course handbook, and your learning resources centre may have them available electronically. It is very important to check before you start, because it is easier for you to make a note of the biblio-graphic references from the beginning. It will also prevent you from inventing your own method, which you may later have to unlearn. It is important not to get too concerned about the differences of approach you may come across. This is what Amil, a Master's student, had to say:

'Just watch and listen to how each
particular tutor wants to have the structure, the
quotation, the references. One tutor may demand endnotes;
others will tell you that endnotes are awful. If your teacher … is
desperately searching for an explanation for all these
contradictions, lean back, chill, smile. There is no use in
searching for sense in this diversity. Look for the
more important things.'

## Citation in the text

In this section we will look at ways of acknowledging all sources of information other than direct quotation. That is a topic that requires careful consideration and has its own section.

- Information-prominent references are placed in brackets at the end of a para-graph or sentence to tell the reader what your ideas are based upon, or after a particular claim or piece of information.

Example: From early childhood, boys and girls are stereotyped into opposing positions (Wilson 2001). This has made it normal for domestic duties to be allocated to the female gender and the creation of a dominant and subordinate group (Bedford 1990).

- You may want to indicate that an idea is based on a number of studies:

New perspectives have been identified in government policy on care of the elderly (Jonas 1995; Bedford 2000; Wilson 2001).
Dates are in ascending order and citations separated by semi-colons.

- In author-prominent sentences, the name may occur naturally in the sentence, then only the date is included in the bracket:

According to Bedford (1995) government policy on the elderly…

- or it may not; in which case you give both:

> In 1995 Wilson claimed in her research into gender issues in electrical engineering training...

- If you are referring to more than one document published by an author in the same year, then a lower case alphabetical denominator is used to identify the particular text:

> (Wilson 1995a)

- If the text you refer to has two authors, both must be included:

> (Wilson and Bedford 1995)

- If the text has more than two authors it is written like this:

> (Bedford *et al.* 2001)

- If no author is given, 'Anon' is acceptable.
- During your research you may come across a reference, in another source, which seems to be useful. As a general rule you should find the original and refer to it directly; after all, there may be times when you find that a passage has been misquoted or taken out of context. Sometimes it is very difficult to find the original because it is in another country or language or is out of print. Your time limit for submission, particularly when writing essays, might prevent you from finding it. In this case you must make it clear to the reader that you are not using the original source. This is done in the text by means of a phrase such as:

> Bedford (1991) cites the work of Wilson (1938) who developed a prototype adding-machine...
> or
> Wilson (1938), cited in Bedford (1991), developed the...
> or
> Bedford (1991), citing Wilson (1938), refers to the development of...

The system above also applies to reference you may make to prefaces, introductions, forewords and afterwords by one author in the work of another.

## The selection and presentation of visual material

You might want to include visual material to enhance your information. The same principles apply as when citing written material. Perhaps you want to illustrate the subject matter being written about, or part or all of it may exemplify the subject matter. Visual material suitable for inclusion in an essay or bibliography includes diagrams, charts, cartoons, photographs, postcards, original artwork and graphics downloaded from the internet. For example, you might wish to include the Salvador Dali picture of The Crucifixion in your research into that subject. You may be writing about Dali or about some aspect of painting that the Dali painting exemplifies. In all cases, the numbering and placing of images within an essay or dissertation require careful planning.

All visual material should be identified and full details about it should be listed in a separate section, either before or after the body of the essay or dissertation, perhaps following, if not actually within the bibliography. Take a look at some illustrated books to see how and where other authors have recorded the visual material they have used. Do not forget to check whether what you want to include is protected by copyright. If it is you, will have to seek permission to use the material. There may be quite severe penalties for you and your academic institution if you fail to do this.

## ◼ Creating your bibliography

As you find authors and other sources of information for your work, it makes sense to create your bibliography from the start of the course. Once you start writing it is crucial that you check each time you make a reference that it is in your bibliography. If you try to do it once you have completed your work you will almost certainly overlook some. At best, it is difficult to remember the full details of the source; at worst, it is seen as poor practice by your lecturer who will most certainly check your bibliography and deduct marks if you are referring in your text to sources that are not there.

Your bibliography will contain all the books, texts, papers and other sources you have used to produce your piece of work, in alphabetical order and by author's surname. Your college or university may have a particular style and there are a number of minor variations. Make sure you know what these are. The Harvard system appears to have become the standard form of referencing at most academic institutions and is used to enable your reader to find the material you used as follows:

- author surname followed by initial, separated by a comma [Smith, A.]
- 'ed.' or 'eds', if an edited work, is placed after the name in parentheses [Smith, A. (ed.)]
- year of publication, in parentheses, follows [Smith, A. (ed.) (1998)]

- title of work, underlined, follows [Smith, A. (ed.) (1998) <u>The Education of Our Children</u>
- 'xx edn', if not the 1st edition, follows in parentheses, followed by a full point or comma [Smith, A. (ed.) (1998) <u>The Education of Our Children</u> (3rd edn).]
- place of publication, followed by a colon, followed by the publisher [Smith, A. (ed.) (1998) <u>The Education of Our Children</u> (3rd edn). London: Greenleaf Books.]

Longer entries may have a hanging indent – the second and subsequent lines are indented. Also note how two authors are cited below:

> Graham, D. and Tyler, D. (1993) <u>A Lesson for Us All: The Making of the National Curriculum</u>. London: Routledge.

Although in your text you write '*et al*'. to indicate that a source has more than two authors, they are all included in the bibliographic reference:

> Taylor, S., Rizvi, F., Lingard, B. and Henry, M. (1997) <u>Educational Policy and the Politics of Change</u>. London: Routledge.

If you have more than one text for an author they appear in date order with the earliest first.

If you have cited an author who has contributed to an edited book, the reference looks like this:

> Greenhalgh, P. (1997) 'The history of craft'. In Dormer, P. (ed.) (1997) <u>The Culture of Craft: Status and Future</u>. Manchester: Manchester University Press.

Sometimes we are referring to an unpublished or lecture presentation:

> Grace, G. (2000) 'The state and the teachers: problems in teacher supply, retention and morale'. Paper presented at Regional Dimensions in Teacher Supply and Retention Conference. University of North London, 19 January. [There is no need to repeat the year as it is given at the start.]
>
> Guba, E. G. (1978) 'Towards a methodology of naturalistic inquiry in educational evaluation'. CSE Monograph Series in Evaluation No.8. Los Angeles, CA: University of California, Centre for Study of Evaluation. [N.B. If a foreign work, it is common to specify the state or country.]

or a newspaper or journal article:

> Hacker, R. G. and Rowe, M. J. (1998) 'A longitudinal study of the effects of imple-
> menting a National Curriculum project on classroom processes'. <u>The Curriculum
> Journal,</u> 9(1), 95–103. [This means Vol. 9, issue 1, pages 95–103. 'pp.' is not
> usually used for journal articles.]
> Hague, H. (1998) 'Fears for future as craft classes are axed'. <u>Times Educational
> Supplement</u>, 3 September, p.25.

Note how the article title is indicated by quotation marks and the journal or
paper is underlined in these examples.

Usually, we do not need to include standard dictionaries and encyclopaedias
in the bibliography. However, on occasion, it is important for the reader to find
your source of information. Where there is no obvious author you cite as much
detail as possible.

> Education Authorities Directory (1995) England: The School Government Publishing
> Co. Ltd.

An electronic reference should indicate not only the website but also the date on
which you accessed it. Here are three examples:

> Robinson, B. <u>End of the World Predictions</u> [On-line]. In Ontario Consultants on
> Religious Tolerance. Accessed 19/7/1996.
>
> Or if the reference is within an on-line journal:
>
> Inada, K. (1995) 'A Buddhist response to the nature of human rights'. <u>Journal of
> Buddhist Ethics</u> [On-line], 2, 9 paragraphs.
> http://www.cac.psu.edu/jbe/twocont.html Accessed 21/6/1995.
>
> Or there may be no other way of defining the information:
>
> http://www.nottingham.ac.uk/education/information-for-students/research-
> ethics/reading-list [accessed 29/3/96].

For a personal e-mail, with attachment:

> Macadam, M. (2004) m.macadam594@concept.ac.uk Fwd. <u>Campus News</u> – sent
> 24/01/04, accessed 25/01/04.

You may have used a CD-ROM:

> Goodstein, C. (1991, September) Healers from the deep. <u>American Health</u> [CD-ROM],
> 60–64. 1994 SIRS/SIRS 1992 Life Science/Article 08A [1995, June 13].

You may want to reference videos, audiotapes, CD-ROMs, television and radio programmes or computer software. The general principles are the same as for books, but if there is no author or obvious title you will have to decide what to use as the keyword and how much detail to give about the programme. An organisation could be used as the keyword. Here are some suggestions:

> Phillips, Trevor (series producer) (1998) <u>Windrush</u>. A series of four documentaries
> shown on BBC2 30/05/1998, 06/06/1998, 13/06/1998 and 20/06/1998.
> (www.bbc.co.uk/education)

A reference to something said in a programme might be:

> 'Phillips, T., BBC2, 13.6.1998' (The use of 'BBC2' in the reference means the reader
> can see that the reference is to a television programme without looking in the
> bibliography).

Another form might be:

> Secret History, 20.7.1998, <u>Witch Hunt</u> television documentary about the trial of Helen
> Duncan in 1944 under the 1735 Witchcraft Act. Shown on Channel 4.

## Referencing computer software

List the author's name, if known, and the date of publication. If no author's name is given, list the title of the software followed by the date of publication. Next list any version numbers or other identifying information, the publication medium, the place of publication and the name of the publisher or distributor.

> WordPerfect, Version 6.1, for Windows (1996) [Computer software]. Ottawa, Ontario:
> Corel.

Some authors use 'ibid.' or 'op.cit.' in their bibliography. Ibid. is short for *ibidem*, which is Latin for 'in the same place'; op. cit. is short for either 'opus citatum' (the work quoted) or 'opere citato' (in the work quoted), to save writing the details of the same book every time they reference it. If you see one of them, it means 'hunt back until you can find the details in a previous reference'. This can be very frustrating for the reader and its practice is discouraged.

Checklist of types of reference sources that should all be acknowledged:

- book by a single author;
- book by more than one author;
- book with no author identified;
- book comprising an edited collection of articles;
- article in an edited collection;
- article (sometimes anonymous) in a work of reference;
- edition by one author of the works (e.g. essays, poems, letters) of another author;
- museum or exhibition catalogue;
- pamphlet;
- item or sequence of items in an anthology;
- conference proceedings edited by one or more editors (published);
- conference proceedings edited by one or more editors (unpublished);
- paper from conference proceedings;
- article in a learned journal;
- article in a newspaper or magazine;
- editorial in a periodical (anonymous or otherwise);
- published letter;
- unpublished letter;
- untitled review in periodical (learned journal or newspaper);
- reference work on CD-ROM;
- periodical article on CD-ROM;
- WWW site (entire site);
- document from WWW site;
- feature film (perhaps on video or DVD);
- e-mail message;
- message from on-line discussion forum or news group;
- article from on-line periodical;
- on-line book (whole text or extract);
- interview (already transcribed/edited into print or not);
- unpublished dissertation;

- map;
- advertisement (film, television or radio);
- television or radio programme;
- audio recording (LP, CD, audio tape);
- audio recording (private);
- work of art (paintings, photographs, etc.);
- art exhibition;
- live performance (concert, play);
- computer program (e.g. game);
- reprinted or republished book;
- specific edition of a book;
- multi-volume work;
- book that is part of a series;
- section of a book;
- chapter of a book.

Check with your tutor whether you should put everything you have used into the bibliography or if you are expected to create a list of key references, which identifies only what has been referred to in your assignment, in addition to a more general bibliography.

In a numbered referencing system, superscript numbers[1] placed at relevant points within the text – ideally at the end of a sentence – correspond to numbered references located at the foot of the page; or sometimes at the end of a chapter or the very end of the essay or dissertation. These numbered notes should contain the same information as detailed above.

## Footnotes and endnotes

You may decide to use numbered notes instead of, or as well as, in-text citation, and there are some reasons why they may be preferable:

- the text is not interrupted by references in brackets;
- bibliographical references can be more detailed; additional comments and extra bibliographical detail can be included.

There is some debate as to whether it is preferable to place them as footnotes at the end of each page or group them together as endnotes at the end of the chapter or book. Indeed there is some argument that says they are unnecessary, and that if they are relevant they should form part of the text. Refer to your tutor to check if your academic institution has specific guidance on this matter.

Footnotes are useful because you can see the additional material without turning pages; on the other hand, too many can look untidy and distracting. Endnotes look tidier, but turning to the end of the chapter or book can be irritating.

### How detailed should footnotes or endnotes be?

There is considerable variation in practice, and scope for individual judgement here. Strictly speaking, you only need to give information to allow the reader to find the reference in the bibliography. In this case, however, you might as well use in-text citations and avoid the bother of footnotes. A more common practice is to give a fairly full reference to a source the first time it is cited, and thereafter refer to it in a suitably abbreviated form, at least over consecutive pages or within the same chapter. The first time a book is referred to or quoted from, it might appear something like this:

> Habermas, J. (1972) <u>Knowledge and Human Interests</u> (2nd edition). London: Heinemann, pp. 49–50.

In a subsequent footnote, the same book might then appear like this:

> Habermas, J. <u>Knowledge and Human Interest</u>, pp. 49–50.

## Why, when and how to use direct quotations

When you were making useful notes from texts or lectures we are sure there were phrases, paragraphs or even whole chapters that summed up your understanding of a particular topic. This is good and bad at the same time. It is good because it helps you to clarify your thoughts, justifies some of your thinking and adds weight to your argument. On the other hand, there is a great temptation not to try to interpret it in your own words but to let the author's words speak for themselves. Used wisely, quotations from relevant sources help to bring your work alive and give it credibility; otherwise it just remains either descriptive or your opinion on the topic. In either case, it must be clear to your reader that you are able to interpret the meaning.

Once again your academic institution may have guidelines on what they consider is an acceptable number of quotations and acceptable length. Usually a quotation of a sentence or two is acceptable; more than that looks bad because it seems you were not able to absorb the information and put it in your own words.

- All quotations must be exact, including any grammatical or spelling errors. You can put [sic] in square brackets at the end of the quotation to indicate that these errors are in the work and they are not yours.
- In general you should not have used more than 5 per cent of your word length in direct quotation.
- Quotations of up to 40 words can be included in the text and you should use single quotation marks to indicate where they begin and end.
- If you leave words out of a quotation you should use three dots (this is called an ellipsis).
- You can add your own words to make the meaning clearer but these must be placed in square brackets. The writing must remain grammatical.
- In every case the page number(s) must be included.

Bedford (2006:22) claimed that, 'student's work was enhanced by citing academic sources accurately' and asked for guidelines to be included in their handbook.

Longer quotations are separated from the text, indented and single spaced. The citation, name, date and page number(s) appear at the end, for example:

University lectures are an economical way of transmitting information but the lectures should be well prepared, rehearsed and supported by audio-visual material, otherwise it becomes the means whereby the contents of the speaker's notes are taken into the student's notes without passing through the minds of either. (Balderdash 1957:42)

## What is plagiarism and how can it be avoided?

In this section of the chapter we will look at the issue of plagiarism and what steps you can take to avoid it. Plagiarism is attempting to present material as if it is your own; that is, not acknowledging the source. As well as written text, this also includes visual and electronic material. Indeed, a number of universities have ways of detecting material that has been cut and pasted from the internet. Worse still, some of the material may be protected by copyright legislation and you could cause yourself and your institution serious problems, legally.

It is important that you check with your tutor and your academic institution's regulations for guidance, because the penalties for plagiarising material can be severe; you could fail the module or have your marks reduced or even be asked to leave the course.

It is unlikely that any of you, in this early stage in your academic career, would jeopardise your opportunities by plagiarising work. However, it is difficult for you to prove that you did so unintentionally. It is therefore important to form good habits from the outset. One of the most common causes of unintentional plagiarism is poor note-taking. Make some rules:

- you will not use the author's words without acknowledging them in your notes as a quotation and writing the page numbers down; and
- you will not write notes that are too close to the author's own words without reminding yourself by putting quotation marks around the 'lifted' words and, again, making full bibliographic references including page numbers.

## The most common forms of plagiarism

- using identical words without acknowledging them as a quotation;
- changing words around but still using a great percentage of the original text without acknowledging them as a quotation;
- paraphrasing, but keeping the format of the original;
- blending pieces of more than one source without acknowledgement;
- citing the source but not acknowledging the unchanged words as quotation;
- using sentences here and there without acknowledging the source;
- failing to include all your sources in the bibliography;
- having someone else write your work for you;
- writing a piece of work with someone else and not acknowledging them.

### ACTIVITY

Look at the following and say if they are examples of plagiarism. Here is the original text:

> The historical research uncovered an astonishing variety of definitions for craft. At one extreme craft was, and still is, understood as skilled practice informed by imaginative, creative and cognitive processes and aesthetic judgement. (Dorbed 2005: 217)

**Example 1**
My research found that there were many definitions for craft. At one extreme it was defined as skilled practice, which uses cognitive processes, imaginative and creative ideas and aesthetic judgement.

> **Example 2**
> Dorbed (2005) identifies a range of definitions for craft, stating that it could be skilled practice, which uses imagination, creative and cognitive processes, together with aesthetic judgement.
> **Example 3**
> Craft can be defined as, 'skilled practice', informed by 'cognitive processes', 'imagination and creativity' and 'aesthetic judgement' (Dorbed 1995, p.217).

Here is some final advice from our foundation degree students:

- 'Always change the writing into your own words or use it as quotes' (Colette).
- 'Try to understand what you are reading and then put it into your own words' (Sandra).
- 'I always tried to write it how I understood it' (Wayne).
- 'I read the texts and then didn't write the essay immediately, so that I was able to recall the points in my own way' (Nick).
- 'I wrote notes in my own words and used a specific colour to underline direct quotes' (Natasha).

# 8 How to manage your time, handle stress and cope with revision and exams

We are going to start this chapter by looking at some time management strategies to try to give you a feeling of control over the many competing deadlines you will have as a foundation degree student. By planning your time sensibly, and then sticking to your plan, you will avoid that panicky feeling of falling behind, or the stress that comes from leaving everything to the last minute. There are many different ways of organising your time. Sadly, there is no single rule that works for everyone. As we asked our students about how they manage time, Philip confessed, 'Don't ask me, I haven't yet managed this'. This chapter will start by looking at Stephen Covey *et al.*'s (1994) ideas of principle-centred time management and then offer you some strategies to plan and organise yourself on a structured basis. The best way to organise yourself is the way that works for you. However, in this chapter we will offer you many ideas that may help you to work out your own system. Our aim is to help you to become more productive in your use of time. This feeling of being in control will build your confidence and you should enjoy your study, work and leisure time even more.

Many students feel that poor time management contributes to a feeling of stress, as do many other pressures, such as the difficulties of combining work and study and balancing the demands of friends and family. We will consider a number of ways you can control your stress and anxiety, and then look specifically at how you can prepare for examinations through effective revision and good exam technique. Our aim is to share with you some lessons from our foundation degree students, to enable you to devise a workable revision plan that meets your needs, allows you to cope with pressure and maximises your chances of success.

## ■ Practical strategies for time management

If you are interested in developing an understanding of time management you are likely to find the work of Stephen Covey useful. Covey, together with A. Roger Merrill and Rebecca R. Merrill, has written *First Things First* (1994), a guide to time management that focuses on issues of importance and urgency. Covey suggests a Time Management Matrix divided into four quadrants:

| Quadrant I | Quadrant II |
|---|---|
| Urgent – Important | Not urgent – Important |
| **Quadrant III** | **Quadrant IV** |
| Urgent – Not important | Not urgent – Not important |

**FIGURE 8.1** Time Management Matrix (*Source*: adapted from Covey *et al.* (1994: 37))

Covey's premise is that we should spend most of our time in quadrant II, the 'Quadrant of Quality', and that many important activities, such as revising for examinations and planning for assignments, only become urgent through procrastination or because we do not do enough planning. By the time the activity becomes urgent, it transfers to quadrant I and this causes us stress. If you think about it, it is true that if you feel constantly driven by deadlines, you will always feel pushed along by the tasks you have to complete, rather than in control of all you have to do. We do, of course, need to spend some time in quadrant I, dealing with important deadlines and unforeseen crises, but by investing in quadrant II time we are taking control of the situation, and gradually the need for urgency diminishes.

As for quadrants III and IV, Covey suggests that quadrant III is the 'Quadrant of Deception' where we are meeting other people's priorities and expectations, rather than our own. Here things are urgent, but not important, so why are we doing them? Usually, the answer is because they are important to someone else. As for quadrant IV, the activities here are not urgent and not important, and Covey describes this as the 'Quadrant of Waste'. In other parts of this book we have suggested the importance of recreational activities. Taking good care of yourself fits into quadrant II, whereas quadrant IV is about mindless time-wasting, not planned and enjoyable time out.

In a survey of quality award-winning organisations in Japan, based on Covey's matrix, the successful high-performing organisations had a significantly different time profile to typical organisations. High-performing companies spent more time doing things that are important but not urgent and significantly less time doing things that are urgent but not important. Of course, we are talking about organisations here, but they are made up of individuals and it is worth reflecting on whether there is something we can learn about the significance of having a degree of clarity about what is really important to us.

| Quadrant I | Quadrant II |
|---|---|
| Urgent – Important | Not urgent – Important |
| 20–25% high performers 25–30% typical organisations | 65–80% high performers 15% typical organisations |
| Quadrant III | Quadrant IV |
| Urgent – Not important | Not urgent – Not important |
| 15% high performers 50–60% typical organisations | Less than 1% high performers 2–3% typical organisations |

**FIGURE 8.2** High-performing and typical-performing organisations mapped onto Covey's Time Management Matrix

Covey's work shows us that we should be spending our time doing things that help us to achieve our own goals and that we, personally, prioritise and value. In this chapter, however, we will be solely considering your degree work. We do appreciate that you will have a number of other important priorities, including friends, family, a spiritual life, paid work, healthcare or caring responsibilities, which will also require your time.

## Review the way you spend your time

Many time management texts suggest you complete detailed logs to identify how you spend your time, and how they can be used to organise yourself more effectively. There is an obvious danger here in that too much time is spent in completing the logs to the last minute. We recommend taking a holistic approach and engaging with the real issue, which is how you can manage your time more effectively. A number of our students struggle with conflicting demands of studying, working, family and personal lives and have identified improved time management on their personal development plan, a process that is covered in more detail in Chapter 9. These students have found the following exercise useful, and many of them have incorporated it into their reflective journal, a process also covered in Chapter 9.

Keep a diary for a week, identifying how you spend your time. Include your weekends and all activities from waking to sleeping. You may find it helpful to carry this around with you. Don't worry about accuracy to the minute, but estimate to the nearest quarter of an hour.

Now think back over the last week and consider where you spent most of your time. Draw a copy of Covey's Time Management Matrix on A4 paper and then write in where each major activity fits in on the importance/urgency grid. What does this tell you about how you are currently managing your time?

Now let us look in more detail at how you could use your time more effectively. You have completed an activity showing how you spent last week. Your next task is to identify the most likely opportunities for making time. Much depends on your own personal preferences, but you could try the following strategies:

- Getting up earlier every day and perhaps studying for an hour before everyone else is awake. Many of our students think this is a successful strategy but you may need to think of another strategy if you are not a 'morning person'.
- Planning to work on a number of evenings a week, but not every night. Unlike the suggestion of working in the mornings, there is not a clear finish time, so you need to be aware of your limits, that is, how long you can study before the effort you make outweighs the benefits.
- Finding time to study in between other activities. This is rarely going to give you high-quality study time but it is helpful to carry around some reading, notes to summarise, an essay title to consider or a small task. In that way you can take advantages of breaks between lectures and meetings or use your travelling time on public transport. This has the additional benefit of keeping your ideas 'alive' until you can get down to longer study.

Colette advises that, 'You will get stressed. Use every bit of time you have and use other professionals to help, like your manager to change work shifts around deadlines.'

It is important to establish some control over your time to enable you to develop a successful routine. So what can you learn about the way you worked last week?

**ACTIVITY**

Pick a time last week when you carried out some study activity. If you didn't study at all, make notes on this task after you have spent a period of time studying. Now consider:

- How long did it take you to get down to the task?
- Did you spend time worrying rather than tackling what needed to be done?
- Were you distracted by other people or unrelated tasks?
- Did you make a plan or list what you were going to do?
- Did you prioritise and complete important work first?
- How long were you able to concentrate on the task?
- Were you studying at the best time for you?

This activity could also form part of your reflective journal (see Chapter 9).

## The big picture: planning your year

You made a start with this activity at the beginning of the book, when we asked you to make a year plan of the major events of the course. You will probably now have more detail about assignment dates, examinations and other deadlines such as presentations, so it is important to update your plan or to make a new one as soon as possible.

**ACTIVITY**

Write up your course timetable for the year and then, in more detail, for the term or semester, as applicable. It is helpful to do this either on a wall planner, a year planner, in an A4-sized diary or by using a software package on your computer such as Microsoft Outlook. You may find it useful to highlight key milestones in colour.

- Mark down the beginning and end of each term or semester.
- Mark dates for the submission of coursework for each module.
- Mark dates for the exam periods.
- Mark key personal dates such as school terms, birthdays, anniversaries, holidays and short breaks.

This activity should help you to identify peak times when you have many demands on your time and, conversely, where you are able to invest more time as you have relatively few other demands. You may find it useful to check your progress against this plan on a regular basis. Remember Covey's idea that you should concentrate on doing what is important, but not urgent, to produce work of the best quality.

## Planning your week

Now you should move on to planning each week. Starting with next week, use your diary to allocate how much time you have and when. Be careful, this time management model needs to be balanced against what you need to achieve. What are really important to you are your outputs, the tasks you complete, rather than your inputs, the time you spend. Otherwise you could find yourself in quadrant IV completing unimportant tasks to make up the time.

---

**ACTIVITY**

Now consider your priorities for the week ahead. First consider the tasks you need to complete.

- Look at the reading you need to do before a particular lecture and schedule this in. It is clearly much better to complete any recommended reading before your lecture. In that way you will have a good understanding of the points your lecturer is making, rather than trying to catch up afterwards, or ignoring the reading completely.

- Look at any assignments coming up that you need to read around. Often your lecturers will give you an idea of how to tackle a particular piece of coursework. Further reading afterwards will consolidate your ideas and help you plan for essays and other assignments.

- Plan for work that is due in shortly. Organise these pieces of work, such as essays and seminar papers, into smaller and less daunting chunks. You need to allocate significant amounts of time to writing and redrafting (see Chapter 6). Writing tasks need the highest quality time and should be attempted when you are most productive, although you may be able to fit your smaller preparation tasks into 'down time'.

- Ensure you do not neglect any of your modules, so make sure you complete something to contribute to each of your areas of study, rather than just the one with the most pressing deadline.

---

Now you have your list, work out your priorities. You are going to have to complete quadrant I tasks without fail, but remember you should be working towards less urgency, and panic, and more strategy and forward planning. Make decisions about when you are going to complete each task, and how long you can afford to spend on this.

**ACTIVITY**

Now complete the plan for your week ahead. Allocate your important and urgent tasks first, then those that have value but which are less urgent. Remember to give yourself some time off to relax and socialise, otherwise you can easily become burnt out. A sample working week is shown for a student working full-time but studying part-time in the evenings and occasional Saturdays.

|      | Monday | Tuesday | Wednesday | Thursday | Friday | Saturday | Sunday |
|------|--------|---------|-----------|----------|--------|----------|--------|
| AM   | work   | work lunchtime, finish reading ch.2 | work | 6–7.30 draft essay | 6–7.30 draft essay | Saturday school at college | 10–12 reading plan next week |
|      |        |         |           | work     | work   |          |        |
| PM   | work   | work    | work      | work     | work   | Saturday school | lunch with parents |
| EVE  | 4.30– 9.30 college | evening off | 6–8 plan essay | evening off | 6.30– 7.30 plan revision timetable | evening out with friends | evening off |

**FIGURE 8.3** Sample study timetable

## Planning your study session

Here we are talking about formal study time, not those tasks that can be fitted into odd moments. You should not spend too long planning here, as there is a danger that this can turn into procrastinating, but before you start each session consider:

- what must be done today, without fail – do this job first; it will give you a sense of achievement, then move on;
- what would be useful to do today, but could wait – is it possible to break this task into manageable portions and achieve part of it?
- is there anything on your list that falls into quadrant III or IV time? Discard any activities that are not urgent and not important. Decide if the tasks in your quadrant III are important to you, in which case this becomes a priority and should be completed;
- when you will finish, and then reward yourself for time well spent by doing something you enjoy.

If your study session isn't working because inspiration is not forthcoming, you may need to be flexible and give yourself a break, and schedule in time later in the week. You need to work at times when you can perform at your best for your study time to be effective. It is not sensible to work until you are exhausted and cannot concentrate; you will make mistakes. So give yourself some time and take proper breaks.

## Ideas for managing stress

Not all stress is bad; we need some stress in our life to help to get things done. We each function best and feel best at our own optimal level of physiological arousal. Too little can lead to boredom and 'rust out'; too much can produce 'burn out', and our ability to cope with the demands of life begins to crumble. The initial excitement you felt at enrolling on your degree perhaps turns to worry or panic, and problems seem insurmountable. Often this is a gradual process that you don't notice until it begins to affect you physically, mentally and emotionally.

Getting your time organised is one of the best ways to reduce stress, but here are some other suggestions you might like to consider:

- Look after your diet. Don't drink too much coffee, tea and fizzy drinks; the caffeine will dehydrate you, making your thinking less clear. Drink plenty of water and eat healthily and regularly; your brain will benefit from the nutrients. Some people like to take a multivitamin tablet to help them through particularly stressful periods.

- Regular moderate exercise will boost your energy, clear your mind and reduce any feelings of stress. Take a walk when things are getting too much. Melissa suggests that you 'create a timetable, but when things get too much then take a break – go for a walk, call a friend'.

- Try out some yoga, tai chi or relaxation techniques. You can buy DVDs or CDs or borrow them from the library. Experiment until you find something that works for you; it could be as simple as a long bath or listening to some music. You will find that it will help to keep you feeling calm and balanced, improve your concentration levels and help you sleep better.

- Exercise some self-belief. You were given a place on the course because people believed you have the ability to succeed.

- It is unrealistic to expect to be perfect. You should aim to do what you can, but keep things in perspective. The phrase 'The best is the enemy of the good' is a useful one to consider here.

- Recognise that periods of high stress will be followed by quieter times.

Julie recommends her 'top tip':

> 'Set yourself some targets. I tend to
> think of it as a horse race with several hurdles. Once I have
> reached a hurdle I reward myself with something – usually a cup of
> tea, bar of chocolate, more chocolate and then a bigger bar of
> chocolate! Eventually you will reach the winning post, but be
> prepared to take some falls along the way.'

## Asking for help

Sometimes you may find that you are overwhelmed by feelings of stress and worry. This is a time when many students drop out as they feel they really cannot cope. It is important that you don't keep everything bottled up; you need to take action and confide in someone. Some ideas on how to take steps to address your problems follow.

### Support available from your teaching staff

If you are really stuck on a piece of work, avoiding the issue won't make the problem go away, and might make it worse. It is important to ask for help from your lecturer or personal tutor as early as possible, but remember that some staff may only have limited time to help you. Before you ask for a meeting, ensure that you have done as much as possible to resolve the issue yourself; then a quick e-mail may be all that is needed. You should:

- read through any guidance you have been given in your handbook, assignment briefs and notes and identify the specific queries you may have;
- discuss the issue with fellow course members – can they throw any light on your difficulties? Tamara suggests you 'link up, have a buddy system, you'll need a pal for times like these';
- complete the work as far as you can and then write up a list of key questions about the problems you want to discuss, in order of priority;
- turn up on time and stick to the point – if you have a scheduled time for an academic or personal tutorial, it is likely that another student will have an appointment following yours, so it is in your own interest to make the best use of the limited time available.

*Help from support services*

If you are feeling so anxious that you are experiencing difficulties in sleeping, and your health is suffering, or your relationships with other people are starting to be affected, then it is important to seek some professional help. You could talk to:

- your own GP and tell them about your concerns;
- a member of the university's counselling service; or
- your student union officer, who will be able to give welfare advice and direct you to other services.

You will have been given information on these services during your induction; they are there to help you and will, in most cases, offer free and confidential support.

## Coping with exams and revision

One of the most common pressure points is the period leading up to examinations, so we will focus on how to reduce anxiety by effective revision and exam technique. From what you have read so far you will understand the need to leave plenty of time to revise, so that you don't get into a situation of having to do last-minute cramming. It is a good idea to start at least six weeks before your examination, and up to two months ahead if you feel particularly anxious. Eduardo suggests, 'Start early to avoid any unexpected complications; it always takes longer than you think'.

Drawing up your revision timetable

You need to think about the following issues in order to draw up your revision timetable.

- Are you going to work with other people? If so you need to check their availability.
- How do you work most effectively? For example, short intensive sessions of less than an hour, or whole afternoons and evenings.
- Make sure you balance the time you have available between the subjects, not neglecting ones you find particularly easy or difficult.
- Which topics are you going to revise? It is unlikely that you will be able to revise everything so you need to make some careful decisions based on past papers, course content and your own particular areas of interest.
- As you use your timetable, make sure you monitor your progress. Do not forget to reward yourself when you complete a topic or at other key points.

Marilyn suggests, 'Focus, start early – an hour or two of work a day really helps. Manage your day; if work has been dreadful then give yourself a night off.'

---

**ACTIVITY**

Draw up your revision timetable for at least six weeks before the exams are due to start. Allocate topics to days, but build in some flexibility.

---

The most effective way to revise is to engage with and understand what you have learned; you will get very little from the process of reading and re-reading your notes. It is a good idea to experiment with several alternative revision techniques so that it is more fun and your motivation to study is high. Here are some ideas for you to consider.

- Summarise your course materials onto index cards, thinking about appropriate headings. Identify definitions, concepts, key points and examples for each topic, then gradually reduce the number of cards you use. Eventually, you only have a few cards, each containing the most important information.
- Work with others from your degree to form a 'revision club'. Here each of you tackles and presents a particular theory or area of knowledge to the rest of the group, even devising possible exam questions for others to answer.
- Always work through questions from past papers if they are available. After revising a topic, answer a question on it, and then compare your answer to your notes. As you get nearer to the exam date it is essential to practise writing answers in the time allocated.

## The night before the exam

It is counter-productive to try and cram in facts the night before an exam. Remind yourself that you have followed a revision programme and have done your best. Then follow the tips below.

- Get your clothes and equipment ready. Check you have a watch, ruler, calculator, spare pens, pencils, rubber and any other permitted equipment. Pack a bottle of water.
- Have a bath to relax.
- Set your alarm clock, giving you plenty of time to get to the exam. Plan to leave much earlier than normal, to take account any transport delays.
- Watch something distracting on the television or read something light, then go to bed at a reasonable time.

## The day of the exam

It is normal to feel nervous but try and relax so that you are able to perform as well as possible. Here are some ideas to help you:

- Have something to eat before leaving home.
- Check exactly where the exam room is and what time you are required. Then get some quiet time by yourself. Remind yourself that you have worked steadily in the time leading up to the exam and that you will have done the best you can, whatever the outcome.
- Avoid last-minute revision as this may leave you feeling muddled and anxious.
- Avoid conversations with others just before the exam; you need to keep focused and positive.
- Follow instructions about what you may and may not take into the exam room. Be particularly aware of the rules regarding mobile phones; these are often banned completely from examination rooms.

## During the exam

- If the desks are numbered make sure you are sitting in the correct place.
- Read the instructions on the front of the paper carefully.
- As soon as you are allowed to write, note down the start and finish time of each question. Allow a few minutes at the start to read through and decide which questions to answer and about five minutes at the end to proofread your answers.
- Read all the questions slowly and carefully. Highlight key words and make sure you understand exactly what you are being asked to do. Check that there are no questions you have missed on the back of the exam paper.
- Decide which questions you are going to answer and then answer your best question first, as this will boost your confidence.
- Always plan your longer answers or essay questions before you start writing. Ensure your answers have a sound structure, and remember to analyse and evaluate.
- Write as clearly and as neatly as you can so that the examiner finds your work easy to mark. If, when you are checking your work, you find you have missed out a word or wish to add in or strengthen a point, add it neatly into the text or as a footnote at the bottom of the page.

- Where appropriate include references to theory, although you will probably not be expected to produce a list of references or a bibliography, unless you are taking an open-book examination.

- Always move on to the next question at the end of the time you have allocated yourself. If you do not answer the correct number of questions, it will be less likely that you will pass.

- If you run out of time for a particular question, or you get really stuck, move on and don't panic; leave sufficient space on your paper so that you can add in points later if there is time. You may find ideas come to you when you are working on something else, in which case make some notes on the back of your examination paper. These can be struck through before you give it in.

- If you do begin to panic at any time during the exam, try closing your eyes and taking several slow deep breaths to calm yourself down. Some people like to focus on positive thoughts: 'I can pass this exam', 'I am well prepared', 'I am calm', while doing some deep breathing.

Finally, after the exam, try and avoid post-mortem discussions with other students if you are feeling anxious about your performance. Just tell yourself you have done the best you can at this stage, and move on.

## References and recommended reading

Covey, S., Merrill, A. R. and Merrill, R. A. (1994) *First Things First*. London: Simon & Schuster.
*For more information about principle-centred time management. Appendix B includes a useful review of time management literature and considers the strengths and weaknesses of different time management approaches.*
The Mind Gym (2005a) *The Mind Gym: Give Me Time*. London: Time Warner Books.
The Mind Gym (2005b) *The Mind Gym: Wake Your Mind Mind Up*. London: Time Warner Books.

# 9 Producing a professional development portfolio

Foundation degrees are concerned with the development and assessment of knowledge and abilities for vocational as well as academic learning. Developing the skill of reflective practice is a fundamental element of being a professional. We are going to look at three activities in this chapter: reflective writing; producing a professional development portfolio; and creating a personal development plan. In some cases you may be asked, as part of your studies, to produce a professional development portfolio that includes a reflective journal and personal development plan. In other cases you may be asked for only one of these.

Reflective writing provides an opportunity for you to think critically about your own learning journey. We are told by our new foundation degree students that they often find this a difficult task as it is different from other forms of writing they have done before. It enables the documentation of your experiences, thoughts, questions, ideas and conclusions. It has benefits in that it offers the opportunity for you to challenge yourself about what you do. It also gives you the objectivity to do things differently and better, without seeing problems as a result of personal inadequacy. Keeping a reflective journal is challenging, but can help you to develop a scholarly approach to your practice and learning. This is an essential feature of studying for your foundation degree.

This chapter considers how you can put together a portfolio. For many years, portfolios have been an important element of education for the visual arts. Those of you who have achieved a National Vocational Qualification will be familiar with the idea of portfolio building. We will think about the contents that may be included across a wide range of curriculum areas for HE study. Foundation degree students we have worked with say that after they have completed their degree, they value their portfolio more than the individual assignments they have undertaken. This is because it is a tangible outcome from, and demonstration of, their learning. Finally, we will explore how to produce a personal development plan to improve your capacity to understand what and how you are learning; to review, plan and take responsibility for it.

## ■ Keeping a reflective journal

### Setting some parameters

When used effectively, reflective writing will support you in making personal sense of a diverse set of experiences. This is particularly important when learning is to be incorporated into everyday practice, as it is in a foundation degree. However, because you are writing about your personal experiences, there are some ground rules and boundaries that need to be set at the beginning of the process. In all cases, before you start to write, you will need to know who will see your reflective journal, and if it will be assessed as part of your qualification. There are issues of confidentiality, just like keeping a personal diary, and it may be better that you do not name individuals, but rather refer to them by their role – 'tutor', 'line manager', 'fellow student' and so on.

---

**ACTIVITY**

Check that you have the answers to the following questions before you start your journal:

- Is the journal part of my assessed work? If so, what are the assessment criteria? Is there a word limit?

- Who will see this writing? Is it just for me? If so, it cannot be assessed. Will the work be seen by a second marker? If so, whom? Could it be seen by an external examiner?

- Is it acceptable to present handwritten work? If you use a standard diary it is likely that your entries will be handwritten unless you have a PDA (Personal Digital Assistant) or use a package like Microsoft Outlook.

- What guidelines are there for content? If you are employed and studying part-time, is there a balance to be struck between reflection on your academic and vocational learning?

---

In the literature regarding reflective practice, the work of Donald Schön is most often cited. Schön, in *The Reflective Practitioner* (1983), writes about reflection having two key components. First, 'reflection *on* action', a retrospective activity looking back after any particular event or task and evaluating current skills, competencies, knowledge and professional practice. Second, 'reflection *in* action', a more dynamic process that takes place during the task or event, and that helps to improve performance by adjusting what we do, what we might term 'thinking on our feet'. This work has been extended by John Cowan (1998) who adds 'Reflection *for* action', where you reflect on and learn from previous activities to inform the planning for the next. Consider these ideas in your own journal and decide at what point you are actually reflecting?

## What could your reflective writing include?

There are many ways of structuring a reflective journal. However, in all cases your tutor is likely to want to see the following.

- An analysis of what went well, why it worked and what you achieved. They will not want a straight description of what happened with no analysis. However you may need to be descriptive, to briefly set the context.
- What could have been better and how you would achieve this. Here you are expected to be honest, knowing what went wrong shows that you have learned from the situation. Try to explain the issue rather than offering excuses or blaming others.
- Any links you can make between the theory you have been studying and what happened in practice.
- What you have learned and will do differently in the future. This could be in the format of a personal development plan (see the final section of this chapter). It could be a brief informal note about the changes you would make and how you will know if you have improved. Susan suggests you try to 'think about something after it happened, what you would have done better or differently'.

As we have seen earlier, the important thing is to start to write your thoughts down. You can edit your ideas later. Lara suggests that you 'look into all aspects of your life. Be clear and write your reflective journal as soon as possible after the incident.' To start you off we have suggested an agenda you might like to follow. As you become more familiar with this type of writing, other questions will come to mind and you might prefer to think more creatively.

---

### ACTIVITY

Your first task is to identify something to reflect upon. Are you concerned about something at work or at college; or are you particularly pleased or interested in an activity? Does a critical incident stand out? For example, when we did this exercise with our students, a number of them chose their feelings on the first day of the course. Now ask yourself a series of questions. These may start you off:

- What happened? What is the current problem or issue? Here you can describe the context and use descriptive rather than reflective writing. It is useful to consider what you were responsible for.
- How did you feel? What were your assumptions? Could your assumptions be challenged?
- How did others feel or react? Did they react in the same way or differently from you? Did their reaction affect you?
- Reflect on the actual outcome – what worked well? Why did it work in this way?
- What were the negatives? What were the reasons for them?
- What could be done differently by you and by others next time? Who could help? How would you summarise what you have learned from this experience?

Christina suggests that you 'Pick an issue and thrash it out. Pick yourself to pieces and argue with yourself. Put in strategies and evaluate their outcomes in further reflections.' Jane advises that:

> 'The art of being reflective is to look at yourself, your week, issues, good points, personal achievements, disappointments, and to summarise. This way you create a diary of growth and personal development.'

## Shaping the journal to suit you: possible ideas for structure

### In the form of a diary

Many students find it helpful to buy a large diary or A4 hardback notebook and to write about their work on a regular basis. This idea works well as a personal learning journey, tracking and documenting an evolving understanding of your work and your study. There are advantages to this method if you use this as your one and only diary and always carry it around. Robbie suggests that you 'Write your diary at work; get a hardback book and carry it around'. However, you do need to ensure that your writing is reflective rather than descriptive. One way around this is to note down incidents as they occur, in your diary, and then consider critically the issues later, following the guidelines in the exercise you have just completed. Lisa advises, 'Don't be descriptive when writing your journal. Go deep into what you are writing and ask yourself "Why?" What can you do about this?'

### In terms of issues and themes

Another approach would be to see if you could integrate different parts of your foundation degree in a holistic manner. A danger of undertaking any modular qualification is that the subjects are seen separately. This approach could be an opportunity for you to see your area of study as a whole and identify common themes across the modules.

One interesting way to organise your journal might be to focus on a pertinent reading from part of your course and again use it to identify themes that will give headings for the sections of your journal rather than using dates. You can experiment with this approach by using the following questions to guide your reflection:

- How does this connect with an aspect of my practice at work or my personal views?
- What could I change in relation to this?
- What would happen if I did?

*An analysis of critical incidents*

A critical incident is an event that impacted either directly on your professional practice or indirectly on the way you perceive something about your career.

---

**ACTIVITY**

The company you work for is about to come under new ownership and restructuring is inevitable:

- Describe the incident as objectively as possible.
- What were the assumptions that you were operating with?
- Is there another way to see this event?
- How do the two explanations compare?
- What could you do differently?

---

*A reflection on your own personal development*

A journal could provide a critical reflection on your learning at work, development activities or on the foundation degree itself. It can be very helpful to focus on feedback you have received on your assignments. If you go through a performance review or appraisal at work, reflect on the perceptions of others.

If you are keeping a professional development journal for assessment, you will probably be asked to produce a separate personal development plan, which is described in the last section of this chapter. However, if this is not part of the requirement for your particular foundation degree you may wish to consider the following questions in your journal:

- What do I need to do to improve the quality of what I do?
- What might I do instead of what I do now?
- What am I doing well that I could develop further?
- What innovation could I introduce?
- What other development activities should I be seeking?

## Producing a professional development portfolio

### Different types of portfolio

What is a portfolio? It can be defined as a structured collection comprising labelled evidence and critical reflection on that evidence. It is produced as part of the process of learning and is presented to show evidence of it. Yet the situation is complicated, and David Baume (2003) identifies a number of different types of portfolio. You may have already produced a portfolio for a National Vocational Qualification or have put together a Record of Achievement (RoA) while you were at school. It is important that you are clear about the kind of portfolio you are required to produce for your course.

## The portfolio as repository

This is a portfolio at its simplest level – a collection of materials, preferably with a structure and an index. This could be as simple as a course file, or kept on-line with the materials stored digitally. If your portfolio is going to be assessed, it is unlikely that a repository-style portfolio will be what is required, although you will obviously need to keep some sort of course file.

## The portfolio for development

David Baume describes this type of portfolio as a compost heap, an image that he intends to convey 'not darkness and odour, but rather something that is refined over time, enriched by addition, reduction and turning over' (Baume 2003:4). In addition to acting as a repository, it can act as your own personal workspace, representing your current state of thinking about your course, collecting materials from a wide range of sources in preparation for production of assignments. This sort of portfolio will be in a constant state of flux, and so needs to be organised and indexed. Again, this is essentially a private portfolio, and unlikely to be appropriate for assessment.

## The portfolio for assessment

This form may well make use of the contents of the development and repository portfolio, but will extend them by commentary and reflection. Your lecturer will expect to see additional annotation of the contents. This may include reflection on feedback from your tutors, mentors and, if appropriate, line managers and peers, to demonstrate how knowledge and understanding have been advanced.

**ACTIVITY**

Before you begin to compile your portfolio you need to find out from your tutor:

- What exactly are the required learning outcomes?
- What guidance is there on presentation and length?
- Is there advice on the form, structure, size and content of the portfolio?
- Does there need to be a bibliography?
- What opportunities for formative assessment will be provided before the portfolio is due in?

- Is there a maximum word length for the critical reflection?
- What assessment criteria will be used?
- Who will see the portfolio? The answer to this question may influence what you want to include.
- Is it possible to see assessed portfolios from former students?

## What to include

Clearly each discipline area has its own characteristic forms of working records and products. If you are a scientist you may produce laboratory reports, engineering students may produce design sheets and social science students reports and essays. The main requirement for the evidence in your portfolio is that it is appropriate to the field of study. It is likely that little or no evidence will be produced specifically for the portfolio. You will be able to gather evidence from work or work placements, during fieldwork or observations, and across all modules of the teaching programme.

What will be written specifically for the portfolio is some form of critical reflection or commentary. This is essential for HE1- and HE2-level work and will make sense of the evidence.

### ACTIVITY

Think about all the possible evidence you could collect that is relevant to your particular vocational area. Then look at the suggestions from our foundation degree in Teaching and Learning Support students in the list below. All students are employed as teaching assistants while they are studying for their degree. Are there any items you now want to add to your list, or any you would take issue with?

Foundation degree in Teaching and Learning Support – possible evidence for professional development portfolio:

| | |
|---|---|
| analysis against Higher Level Teaching Assistant (HLTA) professional standards | person specification for job |
| | photographs of children's work |
| assignments from course modules | photographs of the school |
| audio tapes | probation/appraisal records |
| copies of educational qualifications | references |
| copies of e-mails | staff development records |
| CV | staff newsletters |
| evidence of using IT | results of school surveys |
| feedback from peers and tutors | thankyou notes from children, teachers and parents |
| job description | |
| minutes of meetings | video clips |
| observations of working with children | witness statements |

## Collecting the evidence

If you have completed the activity above, you will have started to formulate your ideas about the contents and structure of your portfolio. It is never too early to begin to collect the evidence. Many of our students started by putting documents into a box file, which is fine, but you do need to start sorting it at an early stage. We are not asking you to become filing clerks, but you need to get organised early enough to make the most of the finished portfolio. Jane suggests that you 'Buy the folder early and immediately divide it up into sections'. Selection is more important than collection.

How should you choose your evidence? Evidence needs to be:

- valid – it demonstrates what you claim it does;
- reliable – you can consistently do what you claim;
- current – it is something you did recently (ask your tutor to define current);
- sufficient – it is enough to demonstrate what you claim;
- accurate – it is what actually happened.

It is important that you label your evidence clearly with, as a minimum:

- title or name, and what the evidence is, if this is not to be immediately clear;
- date of production;
- authors, if you are submitting something produced collaboratively;
- how to access it, if you are producing a portfolio using information technology.

## Think about the structure

An explicit structure and signposting, through an index, are vital, both for you and your tutor. Although you may prefer to be given a template for the structure of your portfolio, this is unlikely to happen, as tutors will be concerned to ensure that you feel a sense of ownership of your portfolio. This includes determining form as well as content. You might find this freedom frustrating, so if you would like some further guidance you could consider the following ideas for structuring the portfolio:

- by time, on a daily, weekly or monthly basis, around a reflective diary and cross-referenced to it;
- around the learning outcomes being demonstrated, with a distinct portfolio section for each learning outcome or assessment criterion to be addressed;
- around underpinning knowledge, professional values or occupational standards if they exist;
- around evidence from all the modules on the foundation degree. In this case you could include a representative sample of your work, together with a critical commentary showing what has been learned from any poor performances, and how that learning has been applied;

- mapping against various work roles carried out on placement or cross-referenced to your job description;
- around an analysis of the knowledge, skills and attitudes required by the person specification for your post.

## Writing a critical commentary

The first part of this chapter has covered writing a reflective journal, and one possible strategy is to cross-reference items of evidence into your journal. What if your assessment does not require a journal, just a portfolio? Refer back to the beginning of the chapter because the techniques for writing your critical commentary are the same, but will not be presented in a diary format.

Assessment will generally start from the critical reflection rather than from the evidence itself. The critical reflection is there to make sense of the evidence, to explain what the evidence shows about what you have learned. You should make appropriate referenced use of theoretical sources. This is expected at HE1 level and, to a greater degree, at HE2 level, where you should consider how you apply theoretical or other ideas from the literature to particular topics, either from your work or study. If you are unsure about what is required, have a look at the SEEC level indicators detailed in Chapter 10 and Appendix 1.

It is a good idea to show your portfolio to your peers and colleagues. The formative assessment process is very important, and they will be able to give you some useful feedback. It is always helpful to see how other people have structured their portfolio, and to ask them why they have done it in that way.

## Creating an e-portfolio

A portfolio can take the form of a website or a CD, or be stored as part of your university's virtual or managed learning environment. In all of these cases clear indexing is particularly important. You should ask for specialist help if you wish to use facilities such as Blackboard or WebCT to create and store your portfolio. These systems have considerable possibilities and, increasingly, you may be able to store and then transfer your data in standard formats between different institutions. However, there are significant technical problems to be solved here and you should take advice on how realistic this is for your own HE institution at this time. You will find some useful advice on the Centre for Recording Achievement's website at www.recordingachievement.org

## Checklist for submission of your portfolio

You may find the following checklist helpful before you submit your portfolio for assessment.

*Is it clear and tidy enough so that the assessor can rapidly understand, analyse and assess it?*

A new lever-arch file, with clear dividers for each section, an index and numbered pages, gives a good impression. Perhaps the best way to achieve this is to give a copy of your portfolio to your mentor and ask him/her for constructive feedback.

*Does it contain only relevant documentation?*

Our view is that a portfolio should be no larger than an A4 lever-arch file; any bigger than that and you have not been sufficiently discriminating about the contents.

*Have you included only photocopies of relevant qualification certificates or items of personal value?*

Although staff should make every effort to safeguard your portfolio, you need to make sure there is nothing in it that cannot be replaced.

*Do you need to get written permission to use any of the evidence or should you make any of the evidence anonymous?*

Particular issues apply when using photographs of children in a portfolio, or indeed in other work. Your course tutor should make you aware of this if you are studying for an education-based foundation degree. Be aware that evidence from work may be of a confidential nature.

*Is the portfolio presented appropriately?*

The details of presentation of written work in Chapter 6 will be helpful here. However, you also need to consider visual presentation; Does the portfolio give the impression you want it to give?

## Using your portfolio after you have finished your degree

*Portfolios to support presentations for interviews*

Increasingly, employers tell us that they want to see what applicants can do as well as what they know. You can use an edited version of your portfolio at an interview for employment or for further study. This will bring to life your experience, qualifications and learning. It should be a much reduced version of your assessment portfolio, containing only the work of which you are most proud. You should always ask in advance if the employer wishes to see it, and then tailor each presentation portfolio to each interview.

*An APEL or continuing professional development portfolio*

You may be able to collate some of your work into a portfolio to claim APEL (Accreditation of Prior Experiential Learning) against occupational or professional standards. In this case you will need to index your work carefully and provide a commentary and evidence to show that all or some of the particular qualification requirements have been achieved. APEL is a rigorous process and requires reflection, analysis and theoretical underpinning to demonstrate what you have learned from your experiences. If you are going to produce an APEL portfolio you need to find out what are the formal requirements of the process and ask what support is available from your academic institution.

You may also be able to use an amended version of your portfolio to demonstrate continuing professional development for the purposes of registration, membership or licensing of a professional body, or you may be able to use it as part of your appraisal scheme at work.

## ▉ Personal development planning (PDP)

The Quality Assurance Agency (QAA), in their publication *Guidelines for HE Progress Files* (2001:8), have defined PDP as 'a structured and supported process undertaken by an individual to reflect upon their own learning, performance and/or achievement and to plan for their personal, educational and career development'. It is therefore highly relevant for foundation degree students, as it is intended to help you to:

- become a more effective, independent and confident self-directed learner;
- understand how you are learning, and relate your learning to a wider context;
- improve your general skills for career and study management;
- articulate your personal goals and evaluate progress towards their achievement; and
- encourage a positive attitude to learning throughout life.

### Resources for personal development planning

Following the Dearing Review in 1997, all HE institutions were expected to provide a form of personal development planning (PDP) for their students by 2005/2006 at the latest. Your first port of call should be your own university, as a number of HE institutions have produced electronic PDP systems. There is also a wide range of resources available.

- The publisher Palgrave has a site called Skills4Study, which provides PDP resources for students (www.palgrave.com/skills4study/pdp/).

The other resources listed here are aimed at HE staff but you may find some interesting advice, proformas and links to other sites so they are worth investigating.

- The former Learning and Teaching Support Network (LTSN) Generic Centre, now accessible through the HE Academy website (www.heacademy.ac.uk), provides a range of papers and case studies on PDP.
- The Centre for Recording Achievement (www.recordingachievement.org) is a national network organisation that supports good practice and the sharing of experience for HE institutions.

## Some ideas for developing your own PDP

### Complete a SWOT analysis

SWOT stands for Strengths, Weaknesses, Opportunities and Threats. Carry out an initial diagnosis of your strengths and areas for further development. What opportunities exist for you to resolve weaknesses and demonstrate your strengths? What threats are there to prevent your development?

---

**ACTIVITY**

Complete a SWOT analysis using the questions in Figure 9.1 as a prompt and including any further thoughts of your own. Consider what actions you will need to take to maximise your development during your foundation degree programme. Write these down; we will use them in your PDP later.

---

### Define yourself through psychometric testing

Psychometric testing is now a common feature of graduate recruitment and it is well worth trying out a range of tests, so that you are prepared if they are used in a selection process. They may also give you some insight into areas for development in your personal development plan. The two main types of tests used are aptitude, also known as ability, and personality.

Aptitude tests are used to measure suitability for a particular type of job, and if you have worked before or are studying for your foundation degree on a part-time basis, you may have experienced this type of testing. Common tests include verbal, numerical and diagrammatic reasoning. Tests are administered under controlled conditions outlined by the British Psychological Society; they are strictly timed and have definite right or wrong answers. Examples of publishers of selection tests include Assessment for Selection and Employment (ASE) (www.ase-solutions.co.uk) and Saville and Holdsworth (www.shlgroup.com).

| STRENGTHS | WEAKNESSES |
|---|---|
| What kind of work experience do I have? | What has held me back in the past? |
| What qualifications do I have? | Are there gaps in my knowledge, |
| Do I have any areas of specialist | qualifications or experience? |
| knowledge? | In what areas do I lack confidence? |
| What skills do I have? | Are there any domestic or family |
| What are my personal beliefs or values? | circumstances I need to consider? |
| How much support do I have from others? | Do I have any health problems or |
| What are my strengths of character? | personal concerns? |
| | What are the weak points of my |
| | character? |
| **OPPORTUNITIES** | **THREATS** |
| Who do I know who could help me | If employed, is my job safe or are there |
| progress? | redundancies at work? |
| Are there opportunities at work/college to | Are there any potential family or |
| develop further? | financial problems? |
| Could I ask to work-shadow other | Are those close to me planning to move |
| colleagues? | away? |
| Can I see a gap in the market? | Are changes in technology in danger of |
| What opportunities exist after my | making my knowledge/skills obsolete? |
| degree? | |
| Can I get sponsorship or a grant for | |
| further development? | |

**FIGURE 9.1** SWOT analysis

Personality tests are intended to gather information about how and why you do things in your own particular way. They are different from aptitude tests in that there are no right or wrong answers – they are designed to look at your style, not ability – and it is important to answer questions accurately and honestly. You may have heard of the test organisations such as the Morrisby Organisation (www.morrisby.co.uk) that are used for careers guidance, or the Myers-Briggs Type Indicator (MBTI), which is frequently used by employers. A shortened version of this can be accessed at www.teamtechnology.co.uk. Another popular instrument is by Meredith Belbin, which looks at team roles. Most university careers services run practice test sessions, and there are some useful links on the Prospects website (www.prospects.ac.uk). Another interesting resource is the Mind Gym's book *Wake Your Mind Up* (2005b), which has ideas for personal development.

---

**ACTIVITY**

Log on to the UK test publisher Saville and Holdsworth's website (www.shldirect.com) and practice some aptitude tests. Look at the feedback you receive. Does this suggest any areas for development? Note that you can also volunteer to take new tests as part of a trial, and receive personal feedback.

---

### *Analyse your job description and person specification*

Look carefully at your job description and accompanying person specification. To what extent do you meet the essential and desirable criteria listed? Consider what current skills need to be maintained or improved. Next consider where you lack confidence or have limitations. Could these be areas you need to include in your own development plan? If possible, ask your personnel department for the details of the post at the next level up. Do these give you areas where you could usefully develop?

### *Analyse yourself against key skills*

Consider the key skills of numeracy (application of number), literacy (communication skills) and information technology (IT). Have a look at the standards produced by the Qualifications and Curriculum Authority (QCA) and map yourself against them (www.qca.org.uk). Do you need to develop any of these key skills to progress further? Also look at the level 3 key skill 'Improving Own Learning and Performance'. How do you rate against this? Does your college offer you an opportunity to be accredited for any of these skills? You will find a sample portfolio for assessment against these standards at www.qca.org.uk/11045.html

## Drawing up your own personal development plan

A sample personal development plan is produced as Figure 9.2; however, you can produce your plan in whatever format you wish. This has been adapted from the materials on the Chartered Institute of Personnel and Development (CIPD) website, (www.cipd.co.uk). There you will find useful examples of completed personal development plans under the section on continuing professional development (CPD).

Personal development does not just happen while you are formally studying; it takes place throughout your life. There are lots of ideas of what you can do after your degree in the next chapter, so it is a good idea to keep your plan on a computer so that it can be regularly updated.

PERSONAL DEVELOPMENT PLAN

NAME: ...............................................................................................................

COVERING THE PERIOD FROM: ...............................TO:.....................................

**Aims** (This should be a general summary of what you want to achieve.)

Think about where you want to be by the end of this period? What about in 5 years' time? You might want to:

● be in employment/self-employment/retired/on maternity leave/on a career break/working part-time/doing a job share
● have been promoted to...
● have changed employment status to...
● be living in...

**Objectives** (These will detail how you will achieve your aim. Make sure they are written in a SMART way, that is, they are Specific, Measurable, Achievable, Realistic and Timed.)

| What do I want/need to learn? | What will I do to achieve this? | What resources or support will I need? | What will my success criteria be? | Target dates for review and completion |
|---|---|---|---|---|
| Clearly describe what you want to learn<br><br>Is this realistic and achievable, but challenging? | Detail the specific actions you are planning<br><br>Plan a mix of activities: work-based; formal development; informal and self-directed learning; activities outside work. | List the costs in time and money<br><br>Whose support do you need to turn this plan into reality – a colleague, manager, mentor, employer, friend? | What will you have learned? This is the measure to show that you have achieved your objectives. This could be a qualification, or NVQ units; being able to put new skills into practice; or improved management effectiveness, e.g. meeting all your deadlines. | Set the timescales by which you intend to have achieved this part of your development plan. Be realistic – small successes achieved will quickly provide motivation towards longer-term goals. |

**FIGURE 9.2** Sample personal development plan (adapted from the CIPD website www.cipd.co.uk). Used by permission.

## ■ Recommended reading

*Written for lecturers, although the advice can be usefully adapted for students. It is available to download on www.heacademy.ac.uk publication CPD027.*

Gray, D., Cundell, S., Hay, D. and O'Neill, J. (2004) *Learning through the Workplace: A Guide to Work-based Learning*. Cheltenham: Nelson Thornes.

*Chapter 7 by Jean O'Neill contains useful information and advice about portfolio building.*

The Mind Gym (2005b) *The Mind Gym: Wake Your Mind Up*. London: Time Warner Books

www.recordingachievement.org

*The website of the Centre for Recording Achievement. Supports the implementation of progress files, professional development planning and e-portfolios.*

## ■ References

Baume, D. (2003) *Supporting Portfolio Development*. York: LTSN Generic Centre.
*Written for lecturers, although the advice can usefully be adapted for students. Available to download on www.heacademy.ac.uk publication CPD027.*

Cowan, J. (1998) *On Becoming an Innovative University Teacher: Reflection in Action*. Buckingham: Society for Research into Higher Education/Open University Press.

Quality Assurance Agency (2001) *Guidelines for HE Progress Files*. Gloucester: QAA.

Schön, D. A. (1983) *The Reflective Practitioner*. New York: Basic Books.

# 10 After the foundation degree: progressing to an honours degree and producing a winning CV

This is the final chapter of the book, and it has a particular focus on what you are going to do next. This could be progression to an honours degree, applying for a new job or considering other opportunities ahead. It builds on the personal development plan you produced in the preceding chapter as part of your professional development portfolio. You may want to come back to these sections at certain times in the future. Our aim is to give you some pointers for your personal and career development.

## What next? Using your careers service

Every educational institution will have a careers advisory service and you should tap into their wealth of professional expertise. As a foundation degree student you will have already made a choice about your vocational area, and many of you will already be employed. However, by completing your degree you will have opened up a wide range of opportunities. Your HE careers service can help point you in the right direction, whether it is towards further academic or professional study, a first step on the career ladder, making a sideways move or gaining a promotion.

### ACTIVITY

Find out the contact details of your careers advisory service. If you are currently studying for your foundation degree at a college of further education you may be enrolled as both a student of the college and a university. If this is the case you should initially investigate both services, although the university HE advisory service may be more appropriate to your needs. Make an appointment now to discuss your future plans. Most careers advisers would prefer to see you at an early stage in your foundation degree, so it is important that you do not wait until you are just about to graduate.

By studying for a foundation degree you will have demonstrated many personal and academic skills. If you have completed a professional development portfolio and action plan, as advised in the last chapter, you will already have a good knowledge of your career-related interests, skills, aptitudes, preferences and goals. This information will be helpful to your careers adviser, and you should take along your personal development plan to the first meeting. Your careers adviser will also find the latest copy of your CV helpful. There is advice on how to prepare a CV later in this chapter. You should complete a draft version of this before your first meeting.

It is also important that you are able to identify, understand and articulate any limitations that may affect your plans.

---

**ACTIVITY**

Think about any barriers to learning that you may have identified at the start of your foundation degree. How many of these now apply? Are there any you need to add to the list? It is important that you share any constraints with your careers adviser, so put this list with your personal development plan and your CV, ready for your first meeting.

---

## ■ Further study: how to find the relevant honours degree course

### Your articulated honours degree

In the first chapter we looked at opportunities for progression to an honours degree. As you now know, each foundation degree must have a designated honours degree to which you are entitled to apply under the process known as articulation. Note that many universities give you the entitlement to apply but you are not guaranteed a place; this may depend on your performance on the foundation degree itself. You should have been given information about this at the very early stages of your foundation degree. Hopefully you have already obtained the answers to the questions. If not, now is the time to find out more.

---

**ACTIVITY**

Ask your course tutor for full details about the articulated honours degree for your foundation degree programme.
Specific questions you should ask are:

- Where is the degree taught? You need to consider whether it is at the same campus, or whether there are other travel arrangements you will need to make.
- When is the degree taught? If you are currently working and studying at the same time, will you need to change your working arrangements? Can some of the degree be delivered by distance or on-line learning?
- Which modules are offered? Are there any optional modules you need to choose?

> - Do you need to gain specific grades, such as merit or distinction, to progress or is a pass grade sufficient?
>
> It is really important that you meet and receive guidance and information from the university staff who will be teaching your honours degree. If you do not already know them, then ask your course tutor to arrange a meeting as soon as possible.

You can take your 240 credit points to any university. However, you may also have to go through a detailed interview and/or Accreditation of Prior Experiential Learning (APEL) process. This is to ensure that the learning outcomes from your foundation degree exempt you from the first two years of the specific honours degree for which you wish to study. Chapter 1 gives you more information on APEL. If you are considering applying to a university other than the one validating your foundation degree, it is essential that you start this process as early as possible. You may also wish to consider using your 240 points to gain credit rating for Open University (OU) qualifications. This may offer more flexible attendance alternatives. If so, you should investigate the OU's credit transfer website (www.open.ac.uk/credit-transfer). You are able to use up to 240 points of transferred credit in a 360-point OU honours degree. It is also possible to gain a 300-point OU degree without honours. However, you may only use 200 points of transferred credit towards this.

## Expectations of studying at HE level 3

One of the main issues for our foundation degree students, before progressing to an honours degree, is whether they have the ability to study at this level. A useful guide is to look at the credit level descriptors for studying at HE3 level, as they explain what is needed in terms of the level of complexity, relative demand and autonomy expected of you on completion of a programme of learning at this level. The SEEC (Southern England Consortium for Credit Accumulation and Transfer) website gives a detailed, although complex, analysis of each individual level.

The SEEC credit level descriptors at HE2 (foundation degree) and HE3 (honours degree) are found at www.seec-office.org.uk/creditleveldescriptors2001.pdf (see Appendix 1). The descriptors are shown under four headings:

(i) the subject-specific development of knowledge and understanding in terms of subject discipline and ethical issues;

(ii) the generic, cognitive and intellectual skills that are expected of all learners as they progress through higher education. These are subdivided into analysis, synthesis, evaluation and application;

(iii) a range of generic key transferable skills – appropriate to all learners – subdivided into group working, learning resources, self-evaluation, management of information, autonomy, communication and problem solving; and finally

(iv) subject-specific practical skills, such as resource management, IT, laboratory techniques, design and creative skills in terms of the application of skills and the autonomy of their use.

---

**ACTIVITY**

Look up the credit level descriptors in Appendix 1. Compare the level descriptors at HE1, HE2 and HE3 and notice how progression is characterised by two important factors. First, the autonomy of the learner, and second, the increasing responsibility that is expected of the learner.

---

It is interesting to learn from the experiences of students who progressed to the University of Plymouth from further education colleges across the South West. In an article entitled 'Accessible higher education: meeting the challenges of HE in FE' (2005), John Dixon and his colleagues describe how their students perceive a 'theme of difference' between being a college foundation degree student and a university honours degree student. This was down to two main factors. First, their concern about poor study skills such as academic writing, research, time management and IT skills. Hopefully, by following the advice in this book, these will no longer be concerns of yours. Second, and more fundamentally, they felt a lack of understanding about what honours degree study involves, particularly:

- the type of language used by university lecturers and their expectations in relation to students' theoretical and analytical understanding;
- the amount of reading expected by university lecturers;
- the degree of self-awareness and self-regulation university lecturers expected from third-year undergraduates; and thus
- the lack of self-esteem they felt in joining the third year as 'university freshers'.

(Dixon *et al.* 2005: 38)

These same students, however, did experience a great deal of success, with 92 per cent of the graduates from the foundation degree progressing to the honours degree programme, and almost 50 per cent of them graduating with upper second class honours. Our experiences have been similar, but if you are changing institutions to study for the honours degree we are sure you will appreciate how important it is to speak to university staff to allay any fears as early as possible. Marilyn advises that you should 'Be proud of your progress and embrace the next stage – you can always ask for help'.

## Producing a winning CV: reflecting on your experiences

As a successful foundation degree student you will have a great deal to offer future employers. You may currently be employed and studying part-time, looking to return to employment or about to apply for your first job. Even if you are currently satisfied at work, you should always have a CV written and ready to tailor to opportunities as they arise. We strongly advise you to produce a CV at this stage in your career as it is a good opportunity to reflect on your recent achievements. A CV will also be a useful addition to your professional development portfolio. It could be a helpful prompt in meetings with careers advisers, HE admissions staff and current and future employers, and may also help you obtain some freelance work. This next section is designed to offer some helpful tips.

### Which personal details should you include?

We will divide the preparation and writing of your CV into several sections, and offer our own views on different styles and content. There is no single right way to produce a CV, and you may disagree with some of our views, but work through each of the sections and then make your own mind up about what to include. Some information will remain static, such as personal details, and other sections will need to be tailored to meet each particular opportunity. Let us start with your personal details. These need to be on every copy you send out.

We recommend that every CV has your:

- full name;
- address (you may need to give both a term-time and home address);
- telephone number. We need to issue a word of warning here; if possible, you need to be in control of this number, and ensure it is answered professionally. If you give your mobile number, be aware that it can ring at any time. Further, an inappropriate answerphone message can destroy your credibility with potential employers.
- e-mail details; if you do not have one, set one up, but, again, be aware of the impact of the use of humour in the address;
- date of birth, rather than age. Although this shouldn't be relevant, particularly given the new age discrimination legislation, we all know that potential employers will try to work it out from when you left school, so on balance our recommendation is to include it, otherwise it may suggest you have something to hide.

You may also want to think about:

- nationality – employers now are required to prove that the people they employ are eligible to work in the European Union. You might want to deal with this by stating your nationality on your CV. Regardless, new employers should ask you to produce your passport or your National Insurance number to prove you are able to work legally, so make sure you can do this;
- marital status – we are not sure that this is relevant to any application, but some of our students say they are proud of their married status, and also want to include details of their children's names and ages. Our advice is to limit such personal information to married/single at the most, but it is your decision.

## Gathering information on education, training and other interests

Now is the time to revisit your qualifications and training, and to really sell your foundation degree qualification. Our preference is for qualifications, and work experience, to be listed from the most recent first, as long as this does not obscure a really impressive achievement. So start with making a note of the full details of your foundation degree. Also, think about whether you can approach your tutor to act as one of your referees for the future. There is some guidance on approaching referees in the next section, which you will need to follow.

Now look back at any other qualifications and certificates you have gained. Ask yourself:

- Did you leave school with the equivalent of a level 2 qualification in English and maths; for example O level, CSE grade 1, GCSE or key skills stage 2?
- Did you gain other qualifications at school?
- Since leaving school, have you gained any other vocational, professional or academic qualifications?

**ACTIVITY**

Now gather together any certificates you can find. Many larger employers ask for copies of relevant certificates and you may need to write to the examining bodies for a replacement if you have lost any. Draft a list of your qualifications in order showing the level, subject, grade and school/college/university attended. Start with your foundation degree and work backwards. You can, and should, edit this list later, perhaps grouping together school qualifications as '4 O levels including English and maths', or 'a good general education', but at this stage it is important to see the whole picture. Some employers' application forms ask for this level of detail so, hopefully, your efforts to search out the information will not be wasted.

You should also consider any training or development courses you have attended through work or on your own initiative over the last few years. These activities may indicate an impressive commitment to your own personal development.

Look through these ideas to remind you of what else you have learned and achieved.

- If you are employed, look back at any appraisal or staff development records you may have – there may be short courses you have attended that you have forgotten about.
- What IT training have you done? Did you gain any certificates? Make a list of IT courses you have attended with their dates and levels.
- What software and operating systems are you currently using, e.g. Windows XP, Office 2003, including Outlook, Word and Excel?
- Have you been trained as a First Aider or Appointed Person? Employers are often impressed by this. Even if your certificate has lapsed it may still be worth including it.
- Do you have a full driving licence? Have you had specialist instruction such as minibus (MIDAS) training?
- Do you have any sports or coaching awards?
- Have you been trained in counselling or youth work?
- If you want to work with children or vulnerable adults, have you received clearance from the Criminal Records Bureau?
- Do you have any foreign language skills? If so, which languages and to what level of fluency?
- Are you a member of any professional organisations?
- Finally, think about your interests, hobbies and any sports you play. List any positions of responsibility you hold or have held in any club or organisation and state what your responsibilities and achievements were.

Now draft a section on your training, based on the information you have gathered above. Again, you may have to edit this later, but you should be positive about your accomplishments.

## Thinking about your work experience

Once again, our advice would be to start with what you are doing now and to work backwards, as employers are probably more interested in your present activities. You do not have to list the full address of your employer on your CV; name and location should be sufficient, but it is worth looking up the full details as sometimes these are requested on application forms. Do not worry at this stage if you have varied, limited or largely unpaid work experience; we will deal with how to present that later. For now let us have a look at the raw material.

Find as much information as possible about your employment over the last few years. If you have been working for many years it is acceptable to summarise your early employment record. Look back and try to put down details of the last ten years or so. In particular, find out:

- the full name, address and telephone number of each of your employers and write a brief description of the service they provide;

- your start date, finish date and final salary, together with the total weekly hours you worked, if part-time. (Note, do not put your salary on your CV – save this for negotiating when you are offered the job);

- job title – did this change over the period of employment?

- and summarise your main responsibilities in each post; if you have a copy of your job description this would be helpful. List any particular achievements, and be specific and positive about skills you developed in the job;

- whether there is a person you can ask to act as a referee, particularly from your more recent work experience. Always seek permission first and, if they agree, give them a copy of your CV when it is completed and keep them in touch with your progress. Find out their correct job title, e-mail and phone number as well as a full contact address.

Depending on your age and experience, you may now have a large file of information, or something very slim indeed. Your work experience may be predominantly unpaid or informal, or you may be looking for your first job. We are sure that when you look back on what you have done, you will be able to offer a useful set of skills that can be transferred to a work environment. Do not overlook or undervalue any unpaid work experience; it is important to add this to the exercise you completed above. In each case, include details of your responsibilities, achievements and skills. You could include:

- any voluntary work for a charity or community-based scheme;
- any period of self-employment;
- unpaid work experience, perhaps as part of a period of study;
- time when you brought up children or cared for a family member; and
- periods of unemployment.

## ▓ Now write your CV

By completing the tasks above you have gathered considerable personal information that we hope will be useful in making future applications, be they for HE, professional memberships or for work. You will need to be able to make any application stand out in a positive way by producing a professional CV. This section will take you through the process. You will need to tailor your CV to each job opportunity, taking note of the knowledge, experience, skills and personal attributes suggested by the job details, particularly if a person specification is included for the post.

### Chronological or skills-based CV?

There are two standard styles of CV – chronological and skills-based – and examples of the layout of each can be found in Figures 10.1 and 10.2. You are likely to be familiar with the layout of a chronological CV, which lists your jobs and education in most recent date order and is useful for showing steady progress. This style may be less suitable for you if you have changed jobs frequently or have gaps in your career history, in which case a skills-based CV could be more appropriate. It is your choice as to whether you place your career achievements or your education and training details first. If you have little work experience it is probably best to sell your achievements as a foundation degree student before giving information on Saturday or vacation jobs.

A skills-based CV highlights your skills and achievements rather than your work or education history. This is particularly strong if you write it considering the requirements of the position you are applying for, as it makes your transferable skills and qualities immediately clear. It is useful if you are not currently in work, wish to change career direction or have had a break or spells of unemployment. However, a number of recruiters state that they suspect skills-based CVs are used to hide patchy work histories, so be aware of this and write strongly about the work experience you have had, be it paid or less formal. Additionally, describe how you usefully filled the periods of unemployment.

NAME
Address
Telephone number
E-mail

PROFILE (if using)


CAREER ACHIEVEMENTS
Job title                        Company name/location              Dates

(details of responsibilities and achievements here)



Job title                        Company name/location              Dates

(details of responsibilities and achievements here)



EDUCATION AND TRAINING
Qualification                    Institution                        Dates

(details of training courses here)



ADDITIONAL INFORMATION
Date of birth                    DD/MM/YYYY



References available on request

**FIGURE 10.1** Layout of a chronological CV

NAME
Address
Telephone number
E-mail

PROFILE (if using)

KEY SKILLS
Title of first skill and description

Title of second skill and description

Title of third skill and description

CAREER SUMMARY

| Job title | Company name/location | Dates |
|-----------|----------------------|-------|
| Job title | Company name/location | Dates |

EDUCATION AND TRAINING

| Qualification | Institution | Dates |
|---------------|-------------|-------|

(details of training courses here)

ADDITIONAL INFORMATION

| Date of birth | DD/MM/YYYY |
|---------------|------------|

References available on request

**FIGURE 10.2** Layout of a skills-based CV

## The optional personal profile summary

A profile is a summary of what you have to offer, and is usually placed at the top of the CV to attract the attention of the person reading it. It should inform your reader of your aims at this stage and what skills you have to offer in relation to them. List your major skills, strengths, personal qualities and achievements. Be specific. Give examples, such as 'good team player', 'excellent written skills', 'versatile', 'able to motivate others'. Stating your career objective at the outset makes your job aspirations clear and may encourage the employer to read further. A profile has advantages and disadvantages. A well-written profile that matches the needs of the employer is useful, particularly if you are sending a speculative CV to a large organisation. Some employers, however, take the view that many profiles are empty hype and, indeed, many are.

Now you should write your CV, either using an on-line form, see first activity below, or using a word processor, as in the second activity.

---

**ACTIVITY**

If you wish to produce your CV on-line, you should use a reputable careers advice service such as learndirect (www.learndirect-futures.co.uk), which offers general careers advice, or www.prospects.ac.uk, the UK's official graduate careers website. For both sites you will need to register. Register following the 'My Prospects' link for this invaluable site for HE students, which provides some excellent guidance on writing CVs and application letters, and interview techniques.

By registering you will be able to produce up to three on-line CVs that you can amend whenever you need. If you have graduated you can even have a free professional careers consultant check your CV and give you personal advice on improving its quality and marketability. This is a one-off service, so you should make sure that the CV you submit is your best effort. You will receive written feedback by e-mail in five working days.

The 'CV Surgery' is only open to you when you have finally graduated, although you can produce and amend your CV on-line at any time.

---

**ACTIVITY**

Write your CV using a word processing package, with clear section headings. If you use Microsoft Office you can have a look at their templates and try them out using the CV wizard.

## Some final words of advice

- Try to keep your CV to two pages of A4 if possible; it will help you select only relevant entries.

- Ensure there is plenty of white space around your CV so that it doesn't look cramped.

- Use a clean, commonly font style such as Arial, Times New Roman or Verdana, and choose a font size that is easy to read (minimum 11 point). Avoid fancy patterns and borders.

- Check your draft thoroughly for spelling and grammatical errors. When you are happy give it to someone else to check and give you feedback. Remember that you will be amending your CV to meet the requirements of each particular job vacancy.

- Print out your CV on a high-quality laser printer using good white, not coloured, paper. Do all your hard work justice and do not be tempted to send out poor-quality photocopies, stuffed into an envelope that is too small.

- Do not include photographs unless completely relevant. This may be appropriate in some cases, such as for jobs in the creative arts, or jobs as models or actors. Photographs are rarely flattering; they allow people to make stereotypical judgements about you, and will add nothing to your application for that job as a trainee accountant.

- Do not include any sort of failure – be it your marriage, business, or being asked to leave a job. In fact, do not include your reason for leaving any job.

## ▤ Completing an application form

Many organisations, of course, prefer to issue a standard application form to help them make an initial selection. As it is often the first point of contact between the applicant and the prospective employer or university. It is important that it is well presented and creates a favourable impression. The principles for marketing yourself in CVs also apply to application forms and covering letters. However, application forms provide a further challenge in that you have to fit the breadth of your experience into a set template.

Some forms also have a daunting open page for you to complete, in which you should write a supporting statement. This is your chance to sell yourself to the organisation, so think about why you are making the application and what you can offer in terms of skills or personal qualities to support your application. If no guidance is given, this section could include evidence of relevant skills and qualities, specific achievements and information about your career motivation.

This will depend on the job specification. Look at the section below on writing covering letters for some more ideas.

## Some helpful points to remember

- Read the whole application form carefully before you start to complete it. Make sure you understand fully what each question is looking for, how to provide a spread of evidence from across your work, life and study in your answers, and note all the word restrictions and instructions.
- Use a separate sheet of paper or, if possible, a photocopy of the form to plan your answers in full. Complete a draft of all the answers first.
- Often the form will request that you use a particular colour ink, usually black, as this aids photocopying for shortlisting and interview panels. Never change the colour of ink you are using half-way through.
- If you are typing the form, always use a standard font such as Times New Roman, Verdana or Arial, and never set the size less than 11 point.
- If you are handwriting your application form, use legible, clear style and always make sure your application form has no spelling or grammatical errors.
- If you are applying on-line on employers' websites, never alter the size or format of the employer's form unless you are clearly given that option.
- Answer all questions fully. If you find that there is insufficient room to give a full answer it may acceptable to continue on a blank sheet of paper that can be attached to the application form, but check first.
- Do not be tempted to cut corners and send a CV as a substitute for some questions, unless the form explicitly states that this is an option. You are being asked to interpret your experiences to meet the needs of the question.
- Similarly, the temptation to cut and paste answers from previous forms can sometimes backfire on you if, for example, the question is slightly different. Employers often notice and are rarely impressed.
- Never leave questions unanswered – if they are not relevant put N/A (not applicable) to show that they have not been overlooked.
- Always make sure you complete any enclosed documents such as Equal Opportunities monitoring or health history forms, if the employer has requested them. Failure to do so might eliminate your application.
- Finally, always retain a photocopy of your application form after you submit it to the employer.

## Writing a letter of application

The main aim of this book is to focus on the study skills you need as a successful foundation degree student. This last chapter has spent time thinking about your future, and, in particular, has concentrated on producing an excellent application form and CV. This section will consider what you should include in a covering letter. Sadly, it is outside the remit of this book to coach you for an interview, whether it is for an HE place or a new job, but we will refer you to some excellent sources of information at the end of the chapter.

The purpose of your letter of application is to get the recipient to read not only your CV, but also to see you as a potential candidate for the post. There are several key points you should consider:

- Make sure you address your the recipient correctly. A personal approach is always preferable, in which case use a formal Mr or Miss/Mrs/Ms, or their correct title and their last name; and use 'Yours sincerely' at the end.

- In your first paragraph you should state why you are writing to them. If the position was advertised, mention the position title and say that you are including your CV. For a speculative letter, state the kind of work you are seeking.

- The main body of the letter should be no longer than three paragraphs, and should refer to the experience and skills needed for the post, being careful not to exclude anything mentioned in the advertisement. You need to make it easy for the employer to match you against any person specification they have.

- Tell them something about your career to date that will attract their interest and build on the information in your CV. It might be an area you specialise in, or a particular interest you have developed while studying for your foundation degree, which is relevant. Explain why you are interested in this type of work, so that you can demonstrate an understanding of what it is likely to involve.

- Next concentrate on the skills you have developed, from working and from your experience as a student. Make sure you cover all the skills mentioned in the advertisement and use positive adjectives like 'well developed' and 'strong', quantifying your statements where possible.

- The final paragraph should ask for the opportunity of a meeting to further the application and indicate your availability to attend an interview.

- Check over the letter for spelling and grammatical errors and check that it expresses your enthusiasm and evidence of research into the position and organisation.

- Generally the letter should be typed in the same font as your CV with an original signature. Occasionally you may be asked to hand-write a covering letter. If so, you should comply with this request.

## ■ Your next steps on the road of lifelong learning

We are, of course, aware that for many people their working or personal lives do not progress along continuous, upward paths. For some, a career has breaks and subsequent returns to paid employment, sideways moves both within and outside organisations, or switches from employment to self-employment and retraining for different careers. Therefore personal planning is not something you do once and then forget; rather, it is an attitude towards your future. We hope this book has instilled the importance of this attitude.

You have reached the end of your reading for this book. We hope that this has given you the confidence to achieve your personal and career development goals, and that your life, both now and in the future, has been enhanced through your understanding of this book's content. Best wishes for your future success!

## ■ Websites to visit for more information

www.connexions-direct.com – aimed at young people aged 13–19 but includes a useful jobs4u careers database.

www.guidancecouncil.com – offers careers information, advice and guidance to adult clients.

www.learndirect-futures.co.uk – provides career assessments that generate job suggestions and a great deal of useful job-hunting information. This is a free service but you need to register to use it.

www.niace.org.uk – the website of the National Institute of Adult Continuing Education that advances the interests of adult learners.

www.prospects.ac.uk – an excellent and comprehensive site for HE students. This should be your first port of call. To get the maximum value you need to register to use the full range of services.

www.windmillsprogramme.com – offers a comprehensive range of exercises and activities based on seven tactics for success developed by the University of Liverpool's Graduate Into Employment Unit.

## Recommended reading

Bishop-Firth, R. (2004) *CVs for High Flyers.* Oxford: How To Books.
*Offers clear and directive advice on writing CVs and examples of different layouts and covering letters.*
www.prospects.ac.uk/downloads/sis/booklets/foundation_degree.pdf
*AGCAS information booklet 'Your Foundation Degree...What Next?' available from HE Careers Advisers or to download.*

## References

Dixon, J., Tripathi, S., Sanderson, A., Gray, C., Rosewall, I. and Sherriff, I. (2005) 'Accessible higher education: meeting the challenges of HE in FE'. *Forward,* **6,** 34–8.

# Appendix 1: SEEC Credit Level Descriptors[1]

## Level 4: HE Level 1

### Development of knowledge and understanding (subject specific)

*The learner:*

- **Knowledge base:** has a given factual and/or conceptual knowledge base with emphasis on the nature of the field of study and appropriate terminology.
- **Ethical issues:** can demonstrate awareness of ethical issues in current areas of study and is able to discuss these in relation to personal beliefs and values.

### Cognitive/intellectual skills (generic)

*The learner:*

- **Analysis:** can analyse with guidance using given classifications/principles.
- **Synthesis:** can collect and categorise ideas and information in a predictable and standard format.
- **Evaluation:** can evaluate the reliability of data using defined techniques and/or tutor guidance.
- **Application:** can apply given tools/methods accurately and carefully to a well-defined problem and begin to appreciate the complexity of the issues.

### Key/transferable skills (generic)

*The learner:*

- **Group working:** can work effectively with others as a member of a group and meet obligations to others (for example, tutors, peers and colleagues).
- **Learning resources:** can work within an appropriate ethos and can use and access a range of learning resources.

1. Copyright © 2003 SEEC. Credit Level Descriptors for Further and Higher Education (0-9541375-4-X). Used by permission. (www.seec-office.org.uk)

- **Self-evaluation:** can evaluate own strengths and weakness within criteria largely set by others.
- **Management of information:** can manage information, collect appropriate data from a range of sources and undertake simple research tasks with external guidance
- **Autonomy:** can take responsibility for own learning with appropriate support.
- **Communications:** can communicate effectively in a format appropriate to the discipline(s) and report practical procedures in a clear and concise manner.
- **Problem-solving:** can apply given tools/methods accurately and carefully to a well-defined problem and begin to appreciate the complexity of the issues in the discipline.

## Practical skills (subject specific)

*The learner:*

- **Application:** can operate in predictable, defined contexts that require use of a specified range of standard techniques.
- **Autonomy in skill use:** is able to act with limited autonomy, under direction or supervision, within defined guidelines.

## Level 5: HE Level 2

### Development of knowledge and understanding (subject specific)

*The learner:*

- **Knowledge base:** has a detailed knowledge of major theories of the discipline(s) and an awareness of a variety of ideas, contexts and frameworks.
- **Ethical issues:** is aware of the wider social and environmental implications of area(s) of study and is able to debate issues in relation to more general ethical perspectives.

### Cognitive/intellectual skills (generic)

*The learner:*

- **Analysis:** can analyse a range of information with minimum guidance using given classifications/principles and can compare alternative methods and techniques for obtaining data.
- **Synthesis:** can reformat a range of ideas and information towards a given purpose.

- **Evaluation:** can select appropriate techniques of evaluation and can evaluate the relevance and significance of the data collected.
- **Application:** can identify key elements of problems and choose appropriate methods for their resolution in a considered manner.

## Key/transferable skills (generic)

*The learner:*

- **Group working:** can interact effectively within a team/learning group, giving and receiving information and ideas and modifying responses where appropriate.
- **Learning resources:** can manage learning using resources for the discipline. Can develop working relationships of a professional nature within the discipline(s).
- **Self-evaluation:** can evaluate own strengths and weakness, challenge received opinion and develop own criteria and judgement.
- **Management of information:** can manage information; can select appropriate data from a range of sources and develop appropriate research strategies.
- **Autonomy:** can take responsibility for own learning with minimum direction.
- **Communications:** can communicate effectively in a manner appropriate to the discipline(s) and report practical procedures in a clear and concise manner in a variety of formats.
- **Problem-solving:** can identify key areas of problems and choose appropriate tools/methods for their resolution in a considered manner.

## Practical skills (subject specific)

*The learner:*

- **Application of skills:** can operate in situations of varying complexity and predictability requiring application of a wide range of techniques.
- **Autonomy in skill use:** able to act with increasing autonomy, with reduced need for supervision and direction, within defined guidelines.

## ▨ Level 6: HE Level 3

### Development of knowledge and understanding (subject specific)

*The learner:*

- **Knowledge base:** has a comprehensive/detailed knowledge of a major discipline(s), with areas of specialisation in depth, and an awareness of the provisional nature of knowledge.

- **Ethical issues:** is aware of personal responsibility and professional codes of conduct and can incorporate a critical ethical dimension into a major piece of work.

## Cognitive/intellectual skills (generic)

*The learner:*

- **Analysis:** can analyse new and/or abstract data and situations without guidance, using a range of techniques appropriate to the subject.
- **Synthesis:** with minimum guidance can transform abstract data and concepts towards a given purpose and design novel solutions.
- **Evaluation:** can critically evaluate evidence to support conclusions/ recommendations, reviewing its reliability, validity and significance. Can investigate contradictory information/identify reasons for contradictions.
- **Application:** is confident and flexible in identifying and defining complex problems and can apply appropriate knowledge and skills to their solution.

## Key/transferable skills (generic)

*The learner:*

- **Group working:** can interact effectively within a team/learning/professional group, recognise, support or be proactive in leadership, negotiate in a professional context and manage conflict.
- **Learning resources:** with minimum guidance can manage own learning using full range of resources for the discipline(s). Can work professionally within the discipline.
- **Self-evaluation:** is confident in application of own criteria of judgement and can challenge received opinion and reflect on action. Can seek and make use of feedback.
- **Information management:** can select and manage information, competently undertaking reasonably straight-forward research tasks with minimum guidance.
- **Autonomy:** can take responsibility for own work and can criticise it.
- **Communications:** can engage effectively in debate in a professional manner and produce detailed and coherent project reports.
- **Problem-solving:** is confident and flexible in identifying and defining complex problems and the application of appropriate knowledge, tools/ methods to their solution.

## Practical skills (subject specific)

*The learner:*

- **Application of skills:** can operate in complex and unpredictable contexts, requiring selection and application from a wide range of innovative or standard techniques.
- **Autonomy in skill use:** able to act autonomously, with minimal supervision or direction, within agreed guidelines.

# Recommended reading

Baume, D. (2003) *Supporting Portfolio Development*. York: LTSN Generic Centre. *Written for lecturers, although the advice can usefully be adapted for students. Available to download on www.heacademy.ac.uk publication CPD027.*

Birley, G. and Moreland, N. (1998) *A Practical Guide to Academic Research*. London: Kogan Page.

Bishop-Firth, R. (2004) *CVs for High Flyers*. Oxford: How To Books. *Offers clear and directive advice on writing CVs and examples of different layouts and covering letters.*

Covey, S., Merrill, A. R. and Merrill, R. A. (1994) *First Things First*. London: Simon & Schuster. *For more information about principle-centred time management. Appendix B includes a useful review of time management literature and considers the strengths and weaknesses of different time management approaches.*

Denzin, N. and Lincoln, Y. (eds) (2000) *Handbook of Qualitative Research* (2nd edn). London: Sage.

Foddy, W. (1995) *Constructing Questions for Interviews and Questionnaires*. Cambridge: Cambridge University Press.

Gray, D., Cundell, S., Hay, D. and O'Neill, J. (2004) *Learning through the Workplace: A Guide to Work-based Learning*. Cheltenham: Nelson Thornes. *Chapter 7 by Jean O'Neill contains useful information and advice about portfolio building.*

Jarvis, M. (2005) *The Psychology of Effective Teaching and Learning*. London: Nelson Thornes.

King, G. (2000) *Punctuation*. Glasgow: HarperCollins. *Clearly written guide, part of the Collins Wordpower series.*

Lashley, C. and Best, W. (2001) *12 Steps to Study Success*. London and New York: Continuum, pp. 175–202. *A clear introduction to what is required in writing a dissertation.*

Microsoft Step-by-Step (2003) *PowerPoint 2003 On-Line-Training Solutions*. Microsoft.

The Mind Gym (2005a) *The Mind Gym: Give Me Time*. London: Time Warner Books.

The Mind Gym (2005b) *The Mind Gym: Wake Your Mind Up*. London: Time Warner Books.

Phythian, B. A. (2003) *Teach Yourself Correct English* (revised by Rowe, A.). London: Hodder & Stoughton.

*Useful, accessible book dealing with rules of and offering advice on using language, including essay, letter and report writing.*

Trochim, W. (2005) *Ethics in Research*. London: Sage.

Truss, L. (2003) *Eats, Shoots & Leaves: The Zero Tolerance Approach to Punctuation*. London: Profile Books.

*A wonderful, yet educational, rant on the use and misuse of punctuation.*

White, B. (2003) *Dissertation Skills for Business and Management Students*. London: Thomson Learning.

www.prospects.ac.uk/downloads/sis/booklets/foundation_degree.pdf

*AGCAS information booklet 'Your Foundation Degree…What Next?' available from HE Careers Advisers or to download.*

www.recordingachievement.org

*Website of the Centre for Recording Achievement. Supports the implementation of progress files, professional development planning and e-portfolios.*

# References

Baume, D. (2003) *Supporting Portfolio Development*. York: LTSN Generic Centre.

Bell, J. (1995) *Doing Your Research Project: A Guide for First Time Researchers in Education and Social Science* (2nd edn). Buckingham: Open University Press.

Berne, E. (1968) *Games People Play: The Psychology of Human Relationships*. London: Penguin.

Brookfield, S. (1995) 'Adult learning: an overview'. *International Encyclopaedia of Education*. Oxford: Pergamon Press.

Buzan, T. (1970) *The Mind Map Book: How to Use Radiant Thinking to Maximize Your Brain's Untapped Potential*. New York: Penguin.

Chartered Institute of Personnel and Deveopment (2006) *Sample Personal Development Plan*. London: CIPD.

Covey, S., Merrill, A. R. and Merrill, R. A. (1994) *First Things First*. London: Simon & Schuster.

Cowan, J. (1998) *On Becoming an Innovative University Teacher: Reflection in Action*. Buckingham: Society for Research into Higher Education/Open University Press.

DfES (2004) *Foundation Degree Task Force Report to Ministers*. Nottingham: Department for Education and Skills.

Dixon, J., Tripathi, S., Sanderson, A., Gray, C., Rosewall, I. and Sherriff, I. (2005) 'Accessible higher education: meeting the challenges of HE in FE'. *Forward*, 6, 34–8.

Eysenbach, G. and Till, J.E. (2001) 'Ethical issues in qualitative research on internet communities'. *British Medical Journal*, **323** (7321), 1103–5.

Gardner, H. (1983) *Frames of Mind*. New York: HarperCollins.

Honey, P. and Mumford, A. (1992) *The Manual of Learning Styles*. Maidenhead: Peter Honey.

Jarvis, P. (1992) *The Paradoxes of Learning*. San Francisco, CA: Jossey-Bass.

Kolb, D. (1984) *Experiential Learning: Experience as a Source of Learning and Development*. Englewood Cliffs, NJ: Prentice-Hall.

QAA (2001) *Guidelines for HE Progress Files*. Gloucester: Quality Assurance Agency.

Qualifications and Curriculum Authority (2004) *National Qualifications*

*Framework.* London: QCA.

Robson, C. (1998) *Real World Research: A Resource for Social Scientists and Practitioners.* London: Blackwell.

Schön, D.A. (1983) *The Reflective Practitioner.* New York: Basic Books.

Stephen, M. (2006) *Teach Yourself Basic Computer Skills.* London: McGraw-Hill.

www.bbc.co.uk/webwise – BBC webwise.

www.campaign-for-learning.org.uk – Campaign for Learning.

www.cipd.co.uk – Chartered Institute of Personnel and Development website.

# Index